ISO 9001: 2015
BACK TO THE FUTURE

ISO 9001: 2015
BACK TO THE FUTURE

A Review of the New ISO Annex SL structure for Certification Standards using the draft ISO 9001: 2015 to explain the changes.

David John Seear

AuthorHouse™ UK
1663 Liberty Drive
Bloomington, IN 47403 USA
www.authorhouse.co.uk
Phone: 0800.197.4150

First Edition 10th December 2014

Note:—This First edition was developed following the revision to ISO 9001 using the new ISO structure for certification standards known as Annex SL Both ISO 9000 and ISO 9001 are to be published in 2015 with ISO 9001:2015 being introduced using the new format.

This is the third book in a series of books that were initially developed from the publication of "Understanding the Audit Trail" published by IRCA Inform Issue 24 on the 10th December 2009. http://www.irca.org/inform/issue24/Seear.html

A similar article is also in www.iso.org/tc176/ISO9001AuditingPracticesGroup on the same date

The previous books: -
- ISO 9001 Audit Trail ISBN 978-1-4772-3489-1 (sc)
- ISO 9000 Family of Standards ISBN 978-1-4772-2640-7 (sc)

Both are also available as e'books: -
ISO 9001 Audit Trail ISBN 978-0-9565100-0-6 (e)
ISO 9000 Family of Standards ISBN 978-1-4771-2640-4 (e)

It is intended that Organisation, Certification Bodies and both Internal and External Auditors obtain benefit from "ISO 9001:2015 Back to the Future" so they can improve their understanding of Annex SL and how it should be used following revisions to ISO standards from 2015.

This document is generic and suitable for any organisation whether they are "ISO 9001 Certified" or not, as it gives guidance on the role of the standards in the "ISO Family of Standards" as defined in ISO 9000:2005 and how ISO 9001 should be used. It includes various proposals one of which is to publish a clear detailed structure for ISO Quality Standards.

The guidance notes, proposals and new definitions may be used as individual training notes to help Organisations improve.

© 2014 David John Seear. All rights reserved.

No part of this book may be reproduced, stored in a retrieval system, or transmitted by any means without the written permission of the author.

Published by AuthorHouse 10/12/2014

ISBN: 978-1-4969-9807-1 (sc)
ISBN: 978-1-4969-9809-5 (e)

This book is printed on acid-free paper.

Because of the dynamic nature of the Internet, any web addresses or links contained in this book may have changed since publication and may no longer be valid. The views expressed in this work are solely those of the author and do not necessarily reflect the views of the publisher, and the publisher hereby disclaims any responsibility for them.

Index

Page	Section	Description
1		Index
1	0.0	General Background
3	1.0	Introduction
7	2.0	Annex SL New ISO structure for standards
18	3.0	ISO Standards, Structure and Awareness
25	4.0	"ISO 9001 Family of Standards" Summary
28	5.0	ISO 9000:2014 Draft Fundamentals and vocabulary
33	6.0	ISO 9001:2008 Purpose and scope
41	7.0	Issues within the "Introduction" section of ISO 9001:2015DIS
53	8.0	Comparison between ISO 9001:2015DIS and ISO 9001:2008 requirements.
63	9.0	Auditing
68	10.0	Improvement
83	11.0	Vocabulary and Definitions
95	12.0	Conclusion

Note: - The above definitions clause 11.0 includes an attempt to get common terms not already defined put into ISO 9000 or even ISO 9000:2015 to ensure a better understanding.

Opinions are those of the author and may not be accepted by all parties.

99	Attachment A	ISO standards structure (reference section Sect 3)
104	Attachment B	Back to Basics 10 LinkedIn questions
110	Attachment C	Concerns raised at CQI Leadership Conference
113	Attachment D	ISO (APG) ISO 9001 Audit Trail December 2009
117	Attachment E	Structured selection of KEY issues
124	Attachment G	Problem sheet
125	Attachment H	Summary of Key concerns

0.0 General Background

This is the third book in a series of books attempting to improve the credibility of "Quality" by highlighting the pivotal role of the "ISO 9000 Family of Standards".

This improvement process began on the 10th December 2009 with the publication of two similar articles entitled "ISO 9001 Audit Trail", one published by IRCA Inform Issue 24 and the other by ISO 9001 Auditing Practices Group (APG). (See Attachment D)

This led to the first edition of a book titled "ISO 9001 Audit Trail" published in March 2010. This has now been superseded by a 2nd edition of ISO 9001 Audit Trail November 2012.

The book explains how **audits cannot be effective if auditors do not understand what the output from a process should be**. It championed the importance of carrying out process audits following an audit trail. Although "Audit Trail" has been recognized by many, including the International Register of Certificated Auditors (IRCA), ISO 9001 Auditing Practices Group (APG) and the United Kingdom Accreditation Service (UKAS), the draft revision to both ISO 9001 and ISO 9000 due to be issued in 2015 has failed to include a definition for "Audit Trail".

This book highlights the importance of structuring the ISO certifiable standards into a common format using Annex SL. This approach will allow easy integration of "Certifiable" standards within any organizations management system if applied correctly.

It reminds all users of the structure and purpose of the "ISO 9000 Family of Standards" and references the importance of the supporting "Requirement Standards", "Guidance Standards" and "Related Standards" and how these standards and other reference documents could be **re-launched** in 2015 through the revision of ISO 9000 and ISO 9001.

ISO 9000 FAMILY OF STANDARDS

The "Core" standard within the "ISO 9000 Family of standards" is ISO 9000 itself.

1.0 Introduction

This book is intended to remind everybody what the changes to the "ISO 9000 Family of Standards" in 2015 could achieve providing the restrictive role of ISO 9001 is understood.

ISO 9001 is one of the best known standards however it is just one standard within the "ISO 9000 Family of Standards". It specifies requirements for a quality management system from agreeing with the customer what they require to delivering the product or service to those requirements. It also covers the related supporting activities where they can affect the intended outcome of meeting customer requirements. All views are the authors and are an attempt to help organisations understand the benefits of the ISO 9000 Family of Standards.

ISO 9001 Certification was introduced to give confidence to both the organization, and their customers that the management system being used is capable of consistently achieving the customer requirements. It goes on to state that within ISO 9001 the term product only applies to product or service intended for or required by the customer. ISO 9001 only covers the statutory and regulatory requirements that the product or service has to comply with, not everything the organisation has to comply with.

It is true that ISO 9001, being a basic generic standard, is capable of being used across all of an organisations business activities and any organisation NOT using the ISO 9001 clauses across all of their business activities is missing out on a very effective management tool.

That said the important thing is to recognize when ISO 9001 clauses are being used outside its restrictive scope when carrying out Certification audits.

KEY 1.1
It is true that the tools, (Clauses) within ISO 9001 may be used by the organization across all of their management activities however, when it is used beyond the restrictive scope of ISO 9001 it can cause confusion. The failure to understand and recognize when

ISO 9001 is used outside its intended scope is the primary cause of misunderstanding.

This restrictive scope allows certification bodies to take a selective sample of orders, find out the requirements for those orders then audit to see if the quality management system being used is able to meet the customer requirements. It ensures that ISO 9001 certification can be totally **objective** as it is judged against its ability to meet the actual customer requirements.

KEY 1.2
The primary purpose of ISO 9001 certification is to allow both the organization and their customers to have confidence that the quality management system being used can consistently provide product or service that meets the customer/specified requirements.

Most organisations will recognise the importance of meeting customer requirements and that is exactly what ISO 9001 was introduced to achieve. If ISO 9001 Certification does not achieve this assurance then the credibility of having a quality management system is undermined.

KEY 1.3
Making changes to ISO 9000 and ISO 9001 in 2015 without having a common understanding of their roles within quality could confuse rather than assist and promote the benefits of quality. (See Attachment B, 10 Back to Basics questions)

1.2 Application

This document explains the purpose of certification using ISO 9001 as the example. It highlights numerous concerns and explains, using ISO 9001 certification, what ISO Certification is all about and highlights areas of confusion. It may be used as a reference document to help understand, in a practical manner, how to use the "ISO 9000 Family of Standards" and the supporting standards. The structure of the standards includes the "ISO 9000 Family of Standards" (Core), "Requirement Standards" (R), "Guidance Standards" (G) and "Related Standards" (R) that help organisations manage their activities. **(See Section 4.0 of this book).** This is a generic book that is hoped will help any organisation revisit the original intended purpose of all the "ISO Series" of standards as identified in Attachment A to ensure that they make the most of what already exists without having to deal with extra requirement being forced into ISO 9001 when they are effectively covered within ISO guidance standards.

ISO 9001 has a specific role and is the quality standard that organisations can be certified to and there should be common understanding about the restrictive scope and what this means.

If all quality professionals had the same understanding it would prevent vested interest forcing their own requirements into certification standards thereby changing the scope to include subjective issues.

KEY 1.4
The quality profession should be able to demonstrate the benefits of an effective management system, without resorting to forcing subjective requirements onto ISO 9001 Certified organisations.

1.3 Scope of this book

This book covers ISO standards and their use but is mainly restricted to quality. The intention is to ask all parties to review what is currently taking place and revisit the scope and purpose of ISO 9001 and the certification against that standard in an attempt to obtain agreement on its role within the "ISO 9000 Family of Standards".

It covers the: -

a) **The Annex SL common structure.** The benefits of having one structure to enable the easy integration of the many standards that organisations can choose to be certified to.

b) **Proposed structure for standards that relate to quality.** The "Core ISO 9000 Family of Standards" namely ISO 9000, 9001 and 9004 together with Requirement Standards Tier 1, Guidance Standards (Tier 2) and Related Requirements Tier 3. It also touches on how other documents or books may be introduced into this structure. (Section 3 and Attachment A)

c) **Use and purpose of the "ISO 9000 Family of standards"** namely, ISO 9000 Fundamentals and Vocabulary, ISO 9001 Quality Management System requirements and ISO 9004 Managing for the Sustained Success of an organisation. All three of which cover the "Core" quality management requirements that may be used by any organisation regardless of size and complexity to help them manage their activities.

d) **Benefit of Improvement** is highlighted by including a simple approach to how important it is to gather information and understand how this may be used to improve an organisations business. In its simplicity it is targeting the small to medium sized businesses.

2.0 Annex SL New ISO structure for standards

This new structure is known as Annex SL prescribes a high level standard structure using identical text headings.

This will allow easy integration of the many certifiable standards where organisations wish to formally apply more than one standard within their business activities. ISO 9001:2015 Draft is used to explain how it may be used.

The Annex SL clauses are headed: -

1. Scope
2. Normative References
3. Terms and Definitions
4. Context of the Organization
   4.1 Understanding the organisation and its content
   4.2 Understanding the needs and expectations of interested parties
   4.3 Determining the scope of the management system
   4.4 XXX management system
5. Leadership
   5.1 Leadership and commitment
   5.2 Policy
   5.3 Organisational roles, responsibilities and authorities
6. Planning
   6.1 Actions to address risks and opportunities
   6.2 XXX Objectives and planning to achieve them
7. Support
   7.1 Resources
   7.2 Competence
   7.3 Awareness
   7.4 Communication
   7.5 Documented information
8. Operation
   8.1 Operational planning and control

9. Performance Evaluation
    9.1 Monitoring, measurement analyses and evaluation
    9.2 Internal audit
    9.3 Management review
10. Improvement
    10.1 Nonconformity and corrective action
    10.2 Continual improvement

(Note: - XXX is replaced by say Quality in ISO 9001, Environmental in ISO 14001 etc)

There are two extra clauses in ISO 9001:2015 compared with ISO 9001:2008, which has eight clauses. Although there are some changes in the basic content covering terminology and interpretation it is mainly clause 4 "Context of an organisation" and how this is interpreted that will affect the new term "Leadership" in clause 5. The content within clause 4 brings the new term "Risk Based Thinking" into play by including the organisations strategic direction plus other issues that will need to be reviewed. This change has meant that the clause covering **Quality Management will be reduced to a sub clause (4.4).**

Clause 9 and 10 Performance Evaluation and Improvement were previously included within the 9001:2008 Clause 8 Measurement, analyses and improvement but these two activities are now being treated as separate entities in their own right.

There are **two clauses covering scope** and this could lead to confusion. Because of this I asked for clarification and been advised of the following: -

Quote: - *"Section 1 of each management standard based on Annex SL defines the scope **of the standard,** the reason the standard itself exists, and its purpose. This is determined by the **standard writers**.*

*Section 4.3 relates to the scope **of the management system**. This sets out the boundaries of management system, what is included and what is not (e.g. the MS applies to one factory in a group structure – that would be defined here). This scope is determined by the organisation not the standard writers."* **Unquote**.

These two scopes are very useful as clause 4.3 **allows the organisation to define the scope** of the management system as it relates to clause 1 scope of the standard. In the case of **ISO 9001 it will be restricted to consistently meeting customer requirements.**

Clause 1 Scope
Covers the intended outcome and the boundaries between which the management system applies. The scope is specific to each standard

Auditors should expect alignment between what the organisation has determined in clause 4.3 and what the standard writers have stated in clause 1.

Note: - The scope in ISO 9001 has not changed. In fact Annex A, Table B.1 in ISO 9001:2015DIS has stated that the term "Product" has been changed to "Product or service" and this is a Major difference.

This is rather overstated as it is quite clear from ISO 9001:2008 ISO clause 3 which states that wherever the term "product" occurs it can also mean "service"" so there is no actual change never mind a major one.

Clause 2 Normative References
This is where other standards relevant and useful to the standard under consideration should be referenced. Unfortunately both ISO 9001 and ISO 14001 have chosen to ignore this clause. By stating: -

"No normative references are cited. This clause is included to maintain clause numbering alignment with other ISO management system standards"

It is this approach that has allowed definitions to be changed without retaining a single central source of reference for definitions. This is, and still should be, held within ISO 9000 for all ISO auditing and quality definitions.

(See section 11.0 on definitions in this book for more concerns over this approach)

This drive to remove the use of "Normative References" may have been inadvertently introduced due to the actual listing of 21 clauses in Clause 3 Terms and definitions within Annex SL Fifth edition.

KEY 2.1: -
The failure to reference ISO 9000 as a normative reference in ISO 9001 removes the central repository for fundamentals and vocabulary.

Clause 3 Terms and Definitions
This is where other definitions applicable to that particular standard itself can be introduced. It can even be used to override the definition used in a "Normative reference" by changing it to suit the needs of that particular standard. This allows the central standard for definitions, ISO 9000 for auditing and quality, to retain the formal central definition for any term. Terms and definitions is where new relevant terms can be introduced specific to that particular standard.

Effective use of the clause "Normative references" means there is no need to put every definition into each new standard and thereby restrict the number of different definitions.

Clause 4 Context of an organisation
This covers what has normally already been considered as it covers what their business activity is all about. It includes external as well as internal issues as it relates to the scope.

Clause 4.3 requires the organisation to determine its own scope defining where the boundaries are set for the organisations management system in other words what is in and what is outside the defined boundaries as they relate to the scope of that particular standard.

KEY 2.2: -
This clause 4.3 in the new ISO 9001 will allow each organisation to look at what, how and when the new terms such as Risk, Opportunity, Interested parties etc could impact on the organisations ability to consistently meet customer requirements. In doing this the organisation can adjust the scope 4.3 so it is specific to their business.

(See the "Spiral of Scope" at the end of this chapter.)

Clause 5 Leadership
Has an emphasis on leadership not just management.

- Top management has to demonstrate involvement in the management system
- The policy has to be made available to all parties and communicated to interested parties
  First glance this seems the same as what has gone before namely policy, organisational roles, responsibilities and authorities, communication etc
- The main difference is that top management has to have a "hands on" involvement and be able to **demonstrate** their commitment to the management system. (See Spiral of Scope)

Clause 6 Planning for the quality management system
After much deliberation this now includes risks and opportunities

- Having highlighted the issues and requirements in clause 4 now is the time to address the risks and opportunities the organisation faces through the planning stage
- How will the organisation prevent or reduce undesired effects.
- How can they ensure they meet the intended output and continually improve?
- This clause puts more emphasis on the planning that is integral to the business

Clause 7 Support
This covers the support needed to achieve the intended output.

- The organisation must supply competent resources
- The need to consider internal and external communication
- The terms documents, documentation and records have been removed
  The new approach is to refer to "documented information"
- It removes the previously perceived need for everyone to have procedures and work instructions

- Everyone should understand the term "documented information" and its broader meaning

Clause 8 Operation
This covers what the organisation is there to achieve

- It addresses both in-house and outsourced processes
- It covers process management including having process criteria, controlling the processes within the criteria, controlling planned change and addressing unintended change as necessary
Whatever is at the heart of the business it goes into clause 8

Clause 9 Performance evaluation
Having carried out the activities within clause 8 it is time to check the performance.

- It covers what, how and when things are monitored, measured, analysed and evaluated
- It includes audits, management reviews which should include deciding on what action should be taken to prevent problems recurring or stop them happening in the first place. (Risk!) If a discipline needs procedures or other documents they can be added as required by the organisation

Clause 10 Improvement
This is where you address non conformity and corrective action

- "Risk and Opportunity" is intended to not only address the above **but prevent things happening (Taking over from Preventative Action from ISO 9001:2008)**
- There is no mention of procedures and work instructions etc but where disciplines consider they are necessary they may be used wherever they are beneficial
- The need to continually improve is a basic premise for all standards using Annex SL

SUMMARY

Simply put the Annex SL gives the structure within which the scope and the normative references together with the definitions that are applicable to that standard are defined. This then requires the organisation to look at what issues affect its business. The organisation then needs to ensure they know what these issues are and how to manage them including, where appropriate, the relevant interested parties that could affect their ability to achieve the intended output taking into account the scope. The quality management system is the responsibility of the organisation and there is no attempt to impose requirements on them as long as the organisation can demonstrate they have thought about and dealt with all relevant issues. Leadership is a key issue for success. It highlights the importance of planning the management system to ensure it is effective. It covers all the supporting issues that can influence the success or failure of their activities. This leads to the actual Operation, planning and control etc. which is currently termed Product/ Service realisation in ISO 9001:2008. It then concludes with an evaluation of the performance that has taken place identifying areas that need improvement.

The two major changes within Annex SL are the importance of "Leadership" clause 5 and how Management responsibility needs to deal with Clause 4 "Context of an organisation".

THE SPIRAL OF SCOPE (HOPE!)
Using ISO 9001:2015DIS

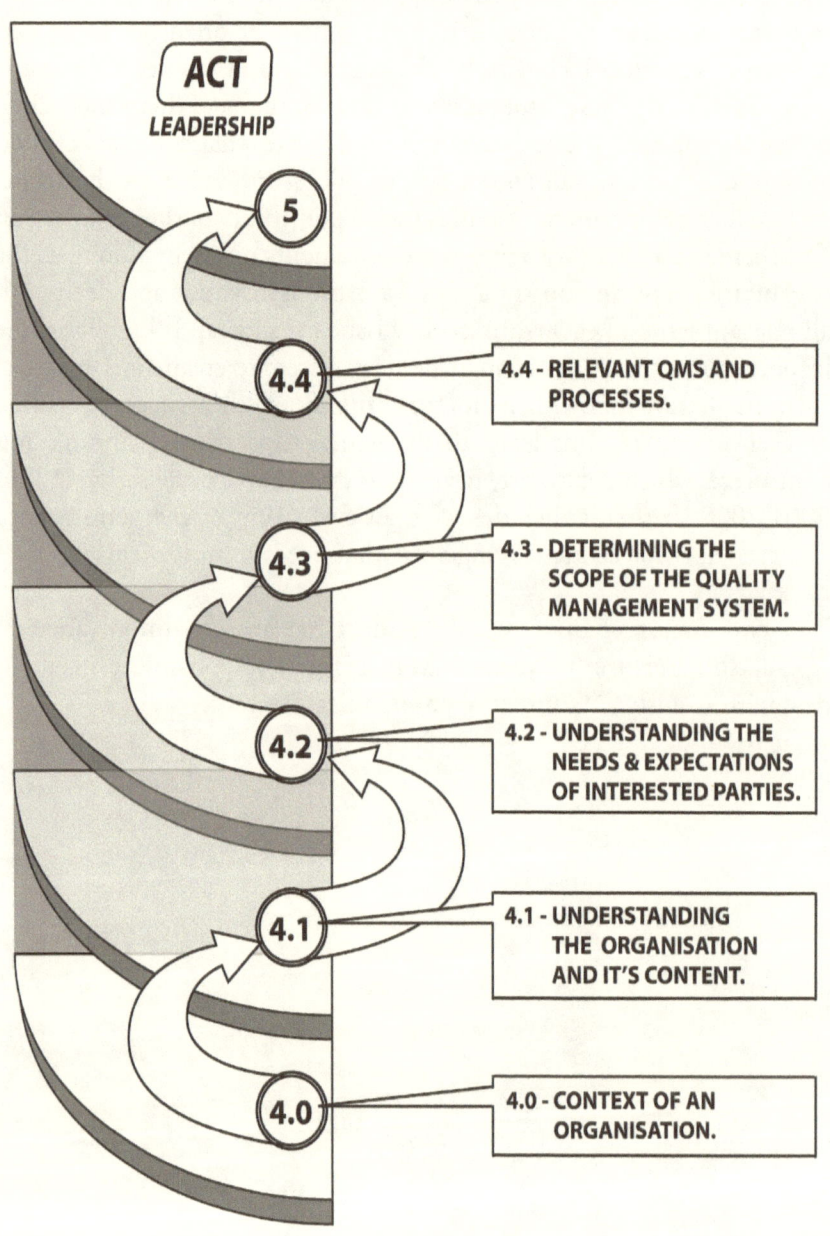

The text in the clauses 4.1 to 4.4 within the "Spiral"

As can be seen from the "Spiral of Scope" the activities within clause 4 underpin the Leadership (Act) part of the Plan, Do, Check, Act (PDCA) process. As already mentioned the most significant changes are in clause 4 which directly leads to "Leadership" clause 5 of ISO 9001:2015DIS.

It should be pointed out that none of this is new. ISO 9001 has always been about looking at risk and identifying what needs to be done to ensure that the organisation is able to consistently meet the customer requirements. What the standard is trying to do is highlight issues that **may** impact on their ability to consistently meet the customer requirements as these might be more important to some organisations than others.

It does however allow the **organisation** itself to decide what, if any of these, internal and external issues are applicable.

4.1 Understanding the organisation and its context
This covers internal and external issues that are relevant to its purpose and its strategic direction. This means anything that can affect its ability to achieve the intended results of the quality management system. This is where once again organisations need to go back to the scope of that particular standard. For ISO 9001 it is the ability to consistently meet the customer and applicable statutory and regulatory requirements

- External – Internal issues
- Strategic direction
- Intended results

4.2 Understanding the needs and expectations of interested parties
This clearly states the importance of taking into account other parties and how they may impact on the organisations ability to consistently provide products and services that meet customer and applicable statutory and regulatory requirements.

- Needs and expectations of interested parties as they affect the scope of the standard

4.3 Determining the scope of the quality management system

This is where the standard clearly states that the organisation determines the boundaries and what is applicable. This is important as the **organisation itself** decides what should be included in the quality management system. From this the organisation can establish its scope.

It states that where a requirement of this standard cannot be applied, this standard shall not affect the organisations ability or responsibility to ensure conformity of products or service.

- The organisation shall determine the boundaries and applicability of the QMS in relationship to the ISO 9001 Scope

4.4 Quality management system and its processes

The intention here is the same as ISO 9001:2008 however there are no longer any specified requirements regarding documents. In fact it now uses the term **"Documented Information"**. It then states that organisations shall **maintain** "documented information" to the extent necessary to support the operation of the processes and **retain** "Documented information" to the extent necessary to have confidence that the processes are being carried out as planned

Conclusion

As can be seen from above the organisation should not try to include every new term used in ISO 9001:2015DIS. What should occur is a sensible evaluation to decide what is applicable and what is not. In fact if an organisation can currently demonstrate that they can consistently achieve customer requirement they may not have to do anything but demonstrate that this is the case.

KEY 2.3 Under no circumstances should any Organisation bow down to pressure to take action on every clause or phrase in ISO 9001:2015 where there is no benefit to the organisation itself.

One final point worthy of note is that there is no need to change an Organisations management system or indeed alter it to come in line with the clause numbering introduced in Annex SL.

KEY 2.4 ISO 9001:2015 clearly states that there is no need for an organisation to change its management system to follow the clause numbering of the revised standard. What the organisation needs to do is ensure the elements within each clause are covered as they relate to their business.

Issues such as Quality Manual and the 6 procedures required by ISO 9001:2008 should not be removed without careful assessment of their need and purpose as the structure of the 2008 management system, when used correctly, is very effective.

The "Spiral of Scope" allows the organisation itself to decide what is applicable and ensure only the issues that are relevant within 4.1 and 4.2 and applicable to their business is included within the scope of the quality management system as defined in Clause 4.3 above

3.0 ISO Standards, Structure and Awareness

There is a lot of confusion as to how all the ISO quality management standards should be structured and used. In fact the ISO structure is currently quite good but needs to be better understood as it is not being used in an effective manner. The proposed structure can be used to cover any quality related standard provided the correct terminology is used in their title. (See below)

The author's contention is that the **"ISO 9000 Family of Standards"** is the **"Core"** set of standards and actually forms the basis of many other quality standards and as such should retain the term the **"Family of Standards"** and be kept at the top of the structure.

ISO 19011 mentioned in ISO 9000:2005 as being part of the "Family" should be dropped and placed with the guidance standards.

There are now many standards that relate to quality. There are not only ISO standards but also other countries standards (e.g. American Standards, European standards, British standards etc). It is up to each individual organisation to choose which of standards are beneficial to their business.

This proliferation of discipline specific **"Requirement standards (Quality)"** is now causing a problem as many quality professionals do not know what they are or how to use them.

In order to put some structure into all these standards the author has proposed that, like a documented structure for the Quality Management System (QMS) below, the ISO standards that relate to quality are also formally structured.

Traditional Documented Quality Structure

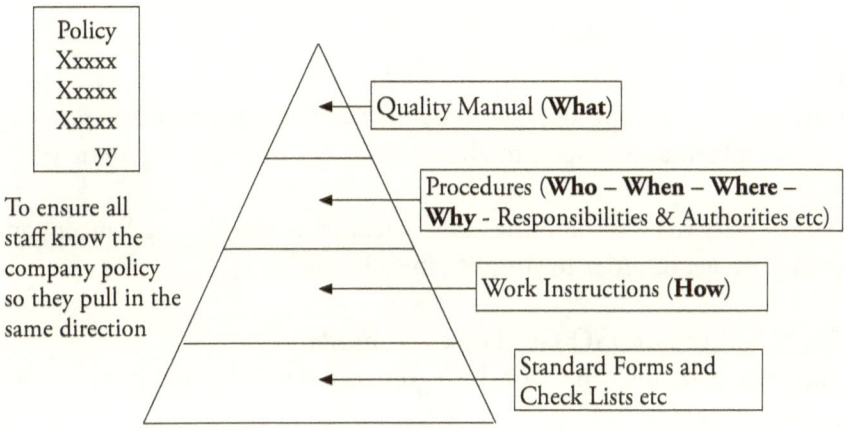

The above is a simple basic structure for a management system and the author would like to propose a clearly defined structure for the many ISO standards that exist in order that organisations can choose the most appropriate standards that will assist them in running their business. Structured in this manner it is easy for organisation to choose which of the tiers below "The "Core ISO 9000 Family of Standards" and others are relevant to their business.

"Core ISO 9000 Family of Standards"
Consisting of ISO 9000, ISO 9001, ISO 9004 and ISO 19011

The "Core" standard is ISO 9000 itself
with the family surrounding it.
Each of the other parts of the "Family" should call
up ISO 9000 as a "Normative Reference"

Tier 1 Sector Specific Requirements
Such as ISO /TC 16949 automotive and ISO 17021 for accreditation bodies A small number but normally a specific requirement for that industry

Tier 2 Formal ISO Guidance Standards
Such as Quality Plans ISO 10005, Risk ISO 31000, ISO 19011 Auditing etc

This covers the multitude of guidance standards that are still growing

Tier 3 Related Standards
Other International or National standards not directly quality related but often industry specific such as Standards that are intended to provide further information useful to an organisations business requirements.

Note: - only the Core and the above Tiers are in the "Flying Saucer" on the next page in order to simplify the approach.

Tier 4 Other non ISO Guidance standards
These relate to any other non ISO guidance standards and can even be country specific

Tier 5 Business books
Often written by Quality Gurus and others that would assist an organisation in managing their business

This structure is nothing to do with their importance but more to do with their application. These five tiers could if utilised effectively assist any organisations or quality professionals to understand how the structure could be used.

NOTE: -
It is not the intention to suggest this structure is what should be used but to encourage others in authority to try to think about an effective structure that could be made available for everyone to buy into. This structure could then be included into ISO 9000:2015. Currently the method of using standards is seen to be unstructured and in many cases poorly understood.

KEY 3.1: -
To ensure there is a clear understanding about the structure and terminology used within the numerous quality standards a listing of standards similar to Attachment A could be included in ISO 9000:2015. This could be kept up to date and readily available through the internet.

The current unstructured approach often means it is not as effective as it could be. The revision scheduled to take place in 2015 would be the ideal opportunity to address this issue. In fact ISO 9000:2015 could be the most appropriate location to add the ISO standards structure as long as ISO 9001:2015 calls up ISO 9000:2015 as a Normative Reference.

KEY 3.2: -
ISO 9001:2015DIS does not call up ISO 9000 as a Normative Reference. This allows each committee to develop their own definitions leading to many different versions. It is this failure to retain ISO 9000 as a normative reference that undermines the fundamentals and vocabulary held in ISO 9000.

3.1 ISO structure for standards

ISO has a specific terminology for standards however this is not always readily understood. This section is an attempt to put some structure into the proliferation of standards and other documents that relate to quality.

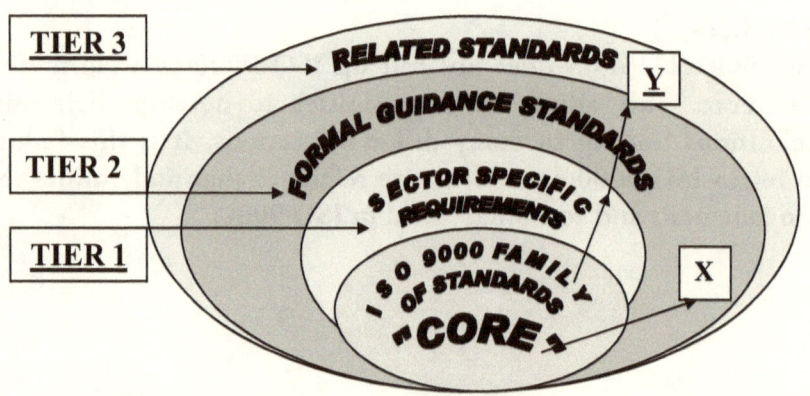

THE FLYING SAUCER

This schematic diagram above illustrates how each organisation can decide what is relevant to their business. It allows a small organisation to choose just ISO 9000 and ISO 9001 from the ISO Family of Standards if that is all they feel they need.

If there are applicable or relevant "Requirement" standards (Usually industry specific) these would be used together with any "Guidance" standards that the organisation decides are appropriate to their business. (See arrow Y)

An Organisation that does not have applicable "Requirement" standards could go directly through to the "Guidance" standards using the (X) route.

The Organisation can choose relevant "CORE" standards plus any of the other Tier 1, 2 or 3 standards as applicable and helpful to their business.

The other "Related" standards such as "Environmental", "Occupational Health and Safety", "Risk" etc are outside the quality standards. Usage would require the organisations management to decide if they were appropriate to their business. (See ISO 9001 clause 0.4 2nd paragraph) Related Requirements (RR) have been included in the example Attachment A.

The whole reason for having all these standards and other documents is to assist an organisation in managing its business. Let's take the well established, documented quality management system that has been shown to be effective and allow that to be the model for a similar but a different layout (The flying saucer). This will help standards to be applied in an easily understood manner.

Let us take each Type one at a time: -

"CORE" ISO 9000 Family of Standards

The "ISO 9000 Family of Standards" is the "Core" and as already stated consists of ISO 9000, ISO 9001, ISO 9004 and currently ISO 19011 although in the author's opinion ISO 19011 should now be placed in Tier 2 Guidance documents and this is indicated in ISO 9001:2015DIS. It should be further noted that the decision to remove the reference to ISO 9000 in clause 2 normative references of ISO 19011:2011 has allowed definitions to be missed, changed and revised with no formal control. (See Auditor in Definition section 11)

In that case the ISO 9000 Family of standards would at least have a clear logic as just three of them would actually be in the "ISO 9000 Family of Standards".

(To be called the "Core" in ISO 9001:2015DIS.)

Tier 1 Sector Specific Requirements

These standards are those that are a requirement. Any standard that is deemed by the industry to be a requirement should fit into this category. The best known of these is ISO/TC 16949 for the automotive industry.

There is however a particular QMS standard that is a requirement and that is ISO 17021 used by accreditation bodies to assess Certification Bodies. There is also AS 9100 Aerospace requirements and although not an ISO standard would easily fit into this structure. In many cases people are unaware of these documents and if a formal structure was agreed the ISO standards could be listed in ISO 9000 in a clear unambiguous manner to help organisations find them. **(See Attachment A)**

It is hoped that with this clearly defined structure it would make them easier to find.

Tier 2 Formal Guidance Standards

This is where the majority of the remaining formal standards reside. There are too many to mention here but **some** of these are in Attachment A of this document.

They cover anything from quality management in projects, customer satisfaction, Quality Plans and many more management issues. These are guidelines and it is up to the organisation to decide if they are applicable. This cannot be done if organisations don't even know they exist.

Tier 3 Management system related documents

These standards are those that are intended to provide further information on specific parts of the management system as deemed to be relevant to the organisations business.

KEY 3.3: - It should be noted that not all these documents are applicable to an organisation and there have been many instances where an organisation has tried to implement one of these methodologies and it has caused them serious problems.

KEY 3.4: - Tier 2 ISO structure of standards covers guidance documents and as such they are not a requirement and it is up to the organisation itself to decide what guidance documents are beneficial.

4.0 "ISO 9001 Family of Standards" Summary (From book of same name)

There are just four documents in the "ISO 9000 Family of Standards" (FoS) defined in ISO 9000:2005 and they each have a different purpose. It is the author's opinion that not fully understanding the purpose and roles of the ISO 9000 (FoS) is the principal reason why ISO 9001, the most commonly used standard, is often misunderstood.

ISO 9000 sets the ground rules and covers the terminology that should be used. It has a pivotal role within the four standards and it is designed to support the other three documents within the family to help any type of organisation manage its business in the most effective manner. It covers the eight management principles developed from the "Vision 2000" findings. It includes the basic fundamentals of a quality management system including the common terms and definitions used in quality.

ISO 9000 is the "backbone" to the "Family of Standards". As such it is important that each standard in the core ISO 9000 Family of Standards should, in their section "Normative References", refer to ISO 9000 as being an applicable reference.

ISO 9001 has a restrictive role; it enables an organisation to demonstrate its ability to consistently provide products that meets customer needs and applicable statutory and regulatory requirements. It covers agreeing with the customer what they require (Agreed Specification), then ensuring the process is planned and managed to ensure those requirements will be met. It should be noted that the statutory and regulatory requirements are only those that relate to that **product** and it is not every statutory and regulatory requirement that an Organisation has to deal with. There are many misunderstandings about ISO 9001 and some of these are covered in this book. In many cases auditors are still being taught to see if the organisations management system has covered all the clauses 4–8 in ISO 9001. This stems from what was called the Document Review where an organisation's Quality Manual is examined to see if it has recognised and addressed all the requirements of ISO 9001 in principle. This "desktop" stage 1 audit is a specific training element from a Lead

Auditor Course. It should be recognised that the Quality Manual is just a stated intent nothing more. It is a commitment explaining "WHAT" an Organisation does. It does not have to cover Why, When, How, Where and Who. The true situation is only revealed, at the levels below the Quality Manual, when a **professional process audit following and audit trail** is carried out to ascertain if the processes that have been put in place can consistently achieve the specified requirements.

How can an auditor ascertain if the process is able to consistently meet the specified requirements if they do not know what the specification for the product is?

ISO 9001 has a restrictive purpose and that is to ensure that the Organisation has a management system that can consistently meet the customer's requirements. It is restricted to the process from enquiry through to delivery of the product. Certification to ISO 9001 is intended to give the Customer confidence that the management system employed by the Organisation can be relied upon to consistently meet the specified requirements.

ISO 9004 is the standard that covers the other requirements that an Organisation has to manage, that have not been addressed by the ISO 9001 standard. It includes "Risk and Strategy" and the whole purpose of ISO 9004, as stated in the title, is managing for the sustained success of an organisation. In other words it covers all the issues outside the scope of ISO 9001 that could affect an organisation's ability to be successful. This is why the whole ISO 9000 Family of Standards (FoS) should be taught, not just ISO 9001.

ISO 9004 is the final part of the Trilogy of standards that enables any Organisation to address the broader quality management issues relating to the sustained success of their business. Where ISO 9001 finishes ISO 9004 fills the gap as it provides a much wider focus on quality management than ISO 9001.

Finally ISO 19011 are the guidelines for auditing management systems. This was previously just for quality and environmental management systems (2002) but the latest ISO 19011 (2011) is generic and suitable for many of the other management system standards that have been published. This standard gives guidance to the auditing activities related to management systems. It emphasises the need to conduct process audits, yet this is still misunderstood in many quarters.

ISO 19011:2011 actually illustrates how things can go wrong when standards are expanded to include other issues. ISO 19011 attempts to cover a much broader range of auditing. In doing this, the original purpose has been lost. This is illustrated by the fact that it states that no Normative References are cited. In other words ISO 9000 is no longer applicable. In this statement alone it has excluded itself from the ISO 9000 Family of Standards.

The four standards (FoS) are all explained with specific examples of how and where they may be utilised and gives organisations an opportunity to decide what stage they are at and which of the four standards are most applicable to their business. The book itself is an attempt to identify how the "ISO 9000 Family of standards" should be used. It identifies some examples of incorrect use and common mistakes made in the interpretation of these standards, in particular ISO 9001. The author does not wish to imply criticism of what is an excellent Family of Standards". Revising a standard on the grounds of improvement when the standards are not used correctly may be counterproductive.

The approach taken with ISO 19011 gives concern over the approach that could be taken over the ISO 9000 and ISO 9001 revision due 2015? This continual drive to add issues that should reside in ISO 9004 into ISO 9001 and the failure to make ISO 9000 a Normative reference in ISO 9001:2015DIS will, if implemented, undermine the whole ISO 9000 Family of Standards and is one of the reasons for this book.

I don't expect all readers to agree with all the views in this book, however, I would request that this book is read with an "Open Mind" leaving preconceived views to one side. I will leave the reader to decide if any of the views and proposals within this document could or should be implemented.

5.0 ISO 9000:2014 Draft Fundamentals and vocabulary

The purpose and scope of ISO 9000 is to act as a "Core" standard within the "ISO 9000 Family of Standards" and this has, in principle not changed. It ensures the fundamentals and requirements are centrally controlled.

ISO 9000 retains its role as the central "Core" of the family (from ISO 9001:2015DIS)

In the ISO 9000:2015DIS it no longer mentions the "ISO Family of Standards" however the four standards previously mentioned in ISO 9000:2005 have, from the statements in ISO 9001:2015DIS, been reduced to three standards and called the "Core". (See above). This is because ISO 19011:2011 has been removed and is located with the guidance standards. Unfortunately ISO 9000 is no longer referenced as a normative reference in ISO 9001:2015DIS. ISO 9000 should retain the "Core" role in the centre of quality and be called up as a normative reference by all standards within the "Family" and any related standard that cover auditing or quality. (Note: - ISO 9000:2005 still used until standards formally revised)

ISO 9000:2005 was called up by ISO 9001:2008 as a "Normative Reference". In fact it stated that ISO 9001:2005 was **indispensable** to the application of ISO 9001.

If this is then related to the ISO structure of standards, see Section 3 "Proposed detailed structure for quality standards", where requirement, guidance and related standards are explained, it can be seen how they support each other.

ISO 9000 helps to ensure there is a common control and understanding of fundamentals, terms and definitions used within all relevant standards.

The ISO 9000 title has not changed and the basic concept is the same however ISO 9000:2014DIS has not retained any obvious link to the current ISO 9000:2005 standard except it still covers the management principles and definitions.

The "management principles" have expanded the content for each although instead of being 8 management principles it has been reduced to 7 management principles. The one missing is the "System approach to management".

However there are some changes to the terms used on four of them. The first 4 are the same except for the change to "Engagement of People". Of the other three one is just "Improvement" another is now "Evidenced based decision making" and then "Relationship management". The 8 management principles previously had a one sentence explanation and the new approach has added over half a page per principle to explain the meaning of the management principles. It gives a one sentence statement, then the rationale, key benefits and actions you can take.

Whenever advising students about making changes to procedures and other documents in the quality management system information should always be given to ensure that the changes to the revision have been made as clear and useful to the user as possible.

This does not seem to be the same approach taken by the ISO standards committees.

For example there are 84 definitions in ISO 9000:2005 and there are around 250 definitions in ISO 9000:2014DIS.

On reviewing the draft standard there is no method of identifying which are new definitions and which have been modified.

(See definitions section of this book for more detail of these concerns)

The question is would it be helpful to the user to be able to see what has changed?

The answer should be yes especially where a definition has been modified.

Taking a sample of definitions relating to audit (Clause 3.10) there are 15 definitions. Seven definitions are the same, four are new (N) with a further four modified (M) yet none are identified as such within the standard.

There are now 250 definitions in ISO 9000 (Draft). It is essential that ISO 9000 should retain its central role and be called up as a Normative Reference for all standards within the "ISO 9000 Family of standards" and others that deal with auditing. Unfortunately this has not occurred and as already mentioned the new draft ISO 9000 now contains no explanation of which standards are part of the ISO 9000 Family of Standards.

(ISO 9001:2014DIS however indicates the family will be called the "Core standards").

ISO 9000:2015DIS Fundamentals and vocabulary introduction

The ISO 9000:2005 introduction has been entirely removed from the ISO 9000:2014DIS. This means there is no reference to the ISO 9000 Family of standards (0.1), the 8 management principles (0.2) the quality management system approach (0.3) process approach (0.4) or Quality policy and quality objectives (0.5) all of which were important issues covered by ISO 9000. However some of these have been moved into the fundamental and vocabulary in ISO 9000 e.g. Management principles or into ISO 9001:2015DIS.

ISO 9000:2014DIS Quality management system – Fundamentals and Vocabulary

The scope has not altered except in the sense that it is taking on a much broader view.

It attempts to make its use more relevant to the 21st century and it moves into Fundamental Concepts where it explains terms beyond the simple definition found in both ISO 9000 and ISO 9001.

Example is the definition for Process 3.6.1: -

- set of interrelated or interacting activities which transforms inputs into outputs.

ISO 9000:2014DIS under "Fundamental concepts" clause 2.2 explains Process approach 2.3.5 by explaining the rational, key benefits and actions that can be taken. It enhances the understanding of ISO 9001:2015DIS and that helps people to understand what things mean and that is why it is surprising that ISO 9001:2015 DIS would indicate that there are no normative references.

KEY 5.1: -
Since 2011 revisions to the "ISO 9000 family of standards" no longer call up "ISO 9000 Fundamentals and Vocabulary" as a "Normative Reference". This makes it difficult to understand the purpose of ISO 9000? In fact the whole role of ISO 9000:2005 is to provide a "Core" standard that explains quality management principles their controls and definitions. ISO 9000 retains the "Definitive" central control for fundamentals and vocabulary and when this is not used within the "ISO 9000 Family of Standards" it undermines the purpose and structure of the Family.

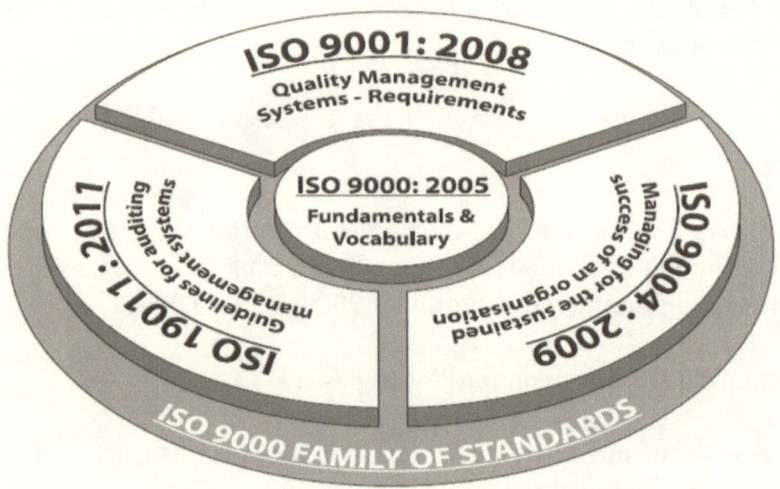

ISO 9000 Family of standards from ISO 9000:2005

The revision for ISO 9001:2015DIS and ISO 14001DIS both fail to call up ISO 9000 as a "Normative" reference. ISO 19011:2011 started this change when it was revised in 2011.

This change is not even defined as a "Major" change yet within ISO 9001:2015DIS Annex A page 44 Table B.1 it indicates that major difference in terminology between ISO 9001:2008 and ISO 9001:2015 is that "Products" has been changed to "Products and Services".

Has no one involved in the revision read ISO 9001:2008 where clause 3 terms and definitions actually states "Wherever the term "Product" occurs it can also mean "Service"?

So in truth it is not even a change never mind a major change.

6.0 ISO 9001:2008 Purpose and scope

The scope in ISO 9001:2008 states that it is an International Standard specifying requirements for a quality management system where an organisation needs to demonstrate its ability to consistently provide product that meets customer and applicable statutory and regulatory requirements. It also requires processes for continual improvement.

Within the Scope Note 1 it states the product only applies to: -

- a) *product intended for, or required by, a customer.*
- b) *Any intended output resulting from the product realisation process*

This helps explains that the "Applicable statutory and regulatory" requirements are only those applicable to the product. This is further illustrated in clause 7.2.1 c) where it states the organisation shall determine the statutory and regulatory requirements applicable to the product.

Combining these points it means that the purpose of ISO 9001 is to ensure that the product or service provided to meet customer requirements complies with any Statutory and regulatory requirements that the product or service has to comply with.

In simple terms it means you cannot provide something to the customer that does not meet the relevant statutory and regulatory requirement applicable to the product or service being provided.

Clause 2 Normative references states that **ISO 9000:2005 is indispensable to the application of ISO 9001:2008.**

ISO 9000:2005 identifies the "ISO 9000 Family of Standards" and states they are: -

ISO 9000 describes fundamentals of quality management systems and specifies the terminology for quality management systems

ISO 9001 Specifies requirements for a quality management system where an organisation needs to demonstrate its ability to provide products that fulfil customer and applicable regulatory requirements

ISO 9004 provide information that considers both the effectiveness and efficiency of the quality management system. The aim of the standard is improvement in performance of the organisation and the satisfaction of the customer and other interested parties.

ISO 19011 Guidelines for auditing quality and environmental management systems.

The **"ISO 9000 Family of Standards"** covers a coherent set of quality management system standards facilitating mutual understanding in national and international trade.

KEY 6.0: - ISO 9001 is one standard within the "ISO 9000 Family of Standards" and it has a role that is restricted to having a quality management system that can consistently meet customer requirements and improve.

ISO 9000:2005 also covers the 8 management principles that were introduced to make the revision to ISO 9001:2000 ensure it met the organisations requirements. This approach was developed by the TC 176 sub-committee that became known as "Vision 2000".

ISO 9000 and ISO 9001 standards are complimented with ISO 9004 as it covers all the issues that need to be addressed in order to achieve sustained success. In simple terms it covers all the issues outside the scope of ISO 9001. That is why they are termed a **"Family of standards"**.

As a family it covers the high level "Core" requirements that a quality management system should cover to ensure sustained success.

ISO 9001 Certification is carried out against the restrictive role of ISO 9001 in that is only covers the management system that directly affect any organization and their ability to consistently provide product that meets the customer and relevant statutory and regulatory requirements.

It has been decided not to cover the clauses 4 – 8 of ISO 9001 in this book as these clauses are the one area that have been taught to the detriment of clauses 1 -3 and the introduction section of ISO 9001:2008. There is however two critical things that should be considered when using the clauses and sub clauses within clauses 4 – 8.

- *It is important to remember to judge each clause against the restrictive scope of ISO 9001 or correct interpretation is impossible.*
- *The second thing to remember is to always look at the main clause and its title before using the sub and sub-sub clauses. On too many occasions clauses are used out of context because the sub clause is used in isolation.*

6.1 ISO 9001:2008 Summary of its role.

Provided chapter (4.0) has been read you will be aware of the restrictive role of ISO 9001. An important thing to be aware of is the "Core ISO 9001 Family of Standards" are the generic set of standards that cover the whole of an organisations requirements regarding quality. ISO 9001 does not cover all of the organisations quality related activities because of its restrictive role. This has not always been taught in an effective manner.

ISO 9001 often misunderstood facts: -

KEY 6.1 covers the quality management system and processes that directly affects the organisations ability to consistently meet the customer requirements. (1.1)

KEY 6.2 the statutory and regulatory requirements are only those requirements that the product or service has to comply with. (1.1 / note 1 and 7.2.1 c)

KEY 6.3 ISO 9000 2005 is indispensable to the application of ISO 9001 2008. (Clause 2)

KEY 6.4 ISO 9001:2008 is generic and intended to be applicable to all organisations and as such does not go into too much detail but

gives clauses that should be considered when deciding what to do, but it is up to the organization to decide to what extent the clauses apply. (Clause 1.2)

KEY 6.5 Whenever the term "product" occurs within ISO 9001:2008 it can also mean "service". (Clause 3)

KEY 6.6 Interpretation of the ISO 9001 standard should be carried out by cross referring back to the product requirement, scope, normative references and terms and definitions.

KEY 6.7 Control of all aspects that can affect the management systems ability to meet the customer requirements e.g. "outsourced" processes. (Clause 4.1 Note 1, 2 and 3)

KEY 6.8 Documentation requirements are clearly defined with just 6 procedures and various records that need to be kept plus whatever the organisation needs (4.2.1 c, d)

KEY 6.9 The basic documentation requirements are quite clear and not onerous. (4.2)

KEY 6.10 The term quality management system does NOT mean a documented management system as you can manage system using competent personnel without resorting to writing a procedure or work instructions for everything. (6.2.2 & 4.2.1d)

NOTE 1: - This last point is to explain to those auditors who state it is not possible to carry out an ISO 9001 audit unless there is a procedure that they are wrong. This insistence that there are procedures for everything is not an ISO 9001 requirement and is bureaucratic.

NOTE 2: -Within the ISO 9001:2008 introduction it **excludes** other management systems such as environmental, occupational health and safety, financial and "RISK" management. (See clause 0.4)

A SIMPLE SUMMARY WHERE MISUNDERSTANDINGS OCCUR

6.2 Last but not least the importance of the introduction within ISO 9001:2008

The Introduction is often ignored and very few courses actually explain what is covered. To understand the standard and how it should be used, it is essential that this information is understood as it effects how the standard should be used. There are just four clauses 0.1 to 0.4 covering just two and a half pages so it is not difficult to read or understand.

The clauses are

0.1 General
Indicates the adoption of a quality management system (QMS) is a strategic decision. It is not the intention to imply the need for uniformity of an organisations QMS as it is influenced by the environmental needs and objectives as they relate to the product/service.

0.2 Process approach
Is used to point out the standard itself promotes adopting a system of processes within an organisation that together with the identification and interactions of these processes within the organisations management systems produces the desired outcome. It points out that this can be referred to as the "Process approach". It brings in the Plan, Do, Check, Act (PDCA)

The revision to ISO 9001:2000 included a restructure of the clauses within the standard to cover the Plan, Do, Check, Act approach to quality considering the 8 management principles.

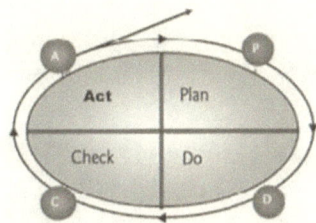

The above is the simple drawing of Plan, Do, Check, Act (PDCA)

PLAN –. Estabilish what needs to be achieved and organise the resources

DO – Implement the processes

CHECK – Monitor and measure the processes and their outputs

ACT – Respond to the findings of the checking activities in order to improve the procces and where necessary reduce the waste

The "Vision 2000" committee, as it became known, was set up to investigate any concerns about ISO 9001. One of the biggest concens was that prior to the year 2000, ISO 9001 was perceived as waiting for things to go wrong before taking any action. This was remedied by restructuring the clauses and introducing clause 8. Measurement, Analyse and Improvement" covering the "Check" "C" from within PDCA. This main clause included both Corrective Action 8.5.2 and Preventative Action 8.5.3 and together with 8.2.2 Internal Audit, 8.3 Control of nonconforming product they became four of the six mandatory clauses required by ISO 9001.

(**Note:** - clause 4.2.3 Control of Documents and 4.2.4 Control of records make up the other two clauses that complete the six mandatory clauses that require a procedure).

The "Vision 2000" revision to ISO 9001 clauses used the Plan, Do, Check, Act approach

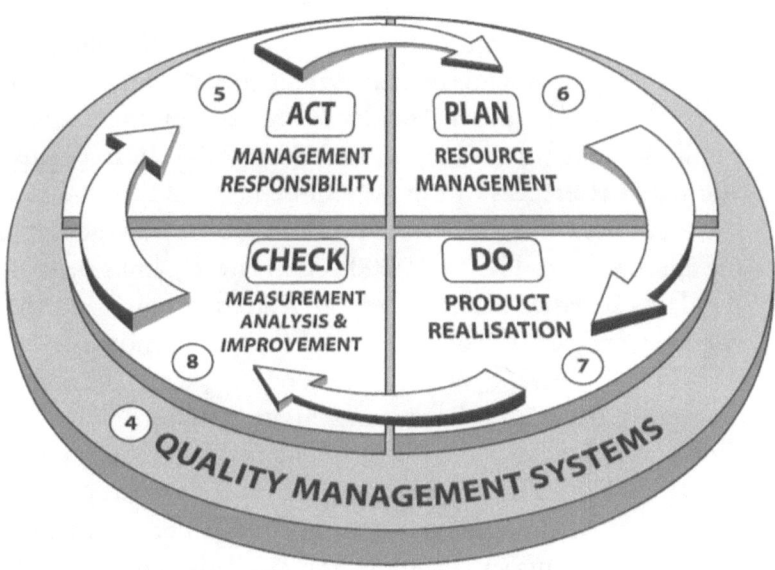

PLAN – Clause 6 Resource management
Establish the objectives and processes necessary to deliver results in accordance with customer requirements

DO – Clause 7 Product realization
Implement the processes

CHECK – Clause 8 Measurement, analyses and improvement
Monitor and measure processes against policies, objectives and requirements for the product and report the results

ACT – Clause 5 Management responsibility
Take actions to continuously improve the process performance.

– Clause 4 Quality management system
As seen from the above figure the quality management system covers all the quality management activities across all the above clauses and supports the PDCA approach.

0.3 **Relationship with ISO 9004**
This covers how the ISO 9001 and ISO 9004 quality management system standards have been designed to complement each other. In fact ISO 9001 has a restrictive role covering the primary process off agreeing with the customer what they require, planning it then using an effective management system to deliver to the agreed specification. These two standards are part of the ISO 9000 Family of standards defined in ISO 9000:2005. In fact clause 2, Normative references within the requirements standard section of ISO 9001 actually states that **ISO 9000:2005 is indispensable** to the application of ISO 9001:2008 so in effect it links these three standards together making them a **"Marched Pair"** and that is why they are part of the "ISO 9000 Family of Standards".

0.4 **Compatibility with other management systems**
This covers how the certifiable standards ISO 9001 and ISO 14001 are becoming more compatible for the benefit of the user community. It also highlights that ISO 9001 does **NOT** include other requirements specific to other management systems, such as those particular to environmental, occupational health and safety, financial or **risk management**
(Note: - Annex SL tries to enhance this common structure for standards that can be certified)

As can be seen from the above it includes some basic tenets that should be recognised when implementing the standard. Unfortunately this information has not always been taught and is the cause of much misinterpretation.

This is why the **introduction** within ISO 9001 is very important as it gives the restrictions and intention of ISO 9001 and how it should be used. It is important to take this into account when interpreting and using the quality management system – requirements of ISO 9001:2008 (Introduction 0.1 to 0.4)

7.0 Issues within the "Introduction" section of ISO 9001:2015DIS

As can be seen from the previous chapters ISO 9001:2008 has a clearly defined restrictive role as specified in its scope. As ISO 9001:2015DIS has the same scope as ISO 9001:2008 both should be **totally objective**, provided it is understood that ISO 9001 is restricted to just the management system being used to consistently meet the agreed customer requirements.

This chapter only covers the **introduction** within ISO 9001 2015DIS.

0.1 **General** This introduces the term "Relevant interested parties" and this could allow a move towards a totally **subjective** approach to ISO 9001. It mentions **"Organisational culture"** and external factors such as **"Socio-economic conditions"** under which it operates.

Key 7.1 Adding subjective issues such as "organizational Culture" and "Socio-economic" conditions when they are not relevant to the scope of ISO 9001 could undermine the purpose of ISO 9001 however clause 4.3 allows the organization to decide what is applicable.

0.2 **The ISO standards for quality management** ISO standards for quality management, has changed the previous term "ISO 9000 Family of Standards" to the "Core" Standards. Why this well established term of "Family of Standards" has been changed to "Core" is not explained. It does however correctly remove ISO 19011 from the "Family" because it is a non **"Core"** Guidance standard. It also highlights the ISO 10000 number range and they are described in Annex C of ISO 9001:2015DIS.

It is suggested that to keep things in line with the previous version the term "Core ISO 9000 Family of Standards" should be used to retain the link to the old term?

KEY 7.2 Changing the term from "ISO 9000 Family of Standards" to just the "Core" standards is one of the many things changed that have lost the link to the previous standard. The term "Core ISO 9001 Family of Standards" might help retain the link to the past where the "Core" itself is ISO 9000.

0.3 **The process approach** again highlights and brings in Plan, Do, Check, Act (PDCA).

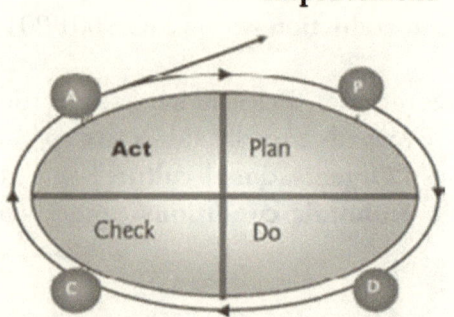

The above is the same simple drawing of Plan, Do, Check, Act (PDCA)

The problem is that the structure of the new draft figure 1 now brings in new terminology that distorts the logic behind the revision of the clauses made in ISO 9001:2000. The clauses used are now 5, 6, 8, and 9. It also indicates that clause 4.4 QMS and process approach are bought in under clause 5 Leadership.

<u>The new terminology within ISO 9001:2015</u>

PLAN **– Clause 6 Planning (Was resource management clause 6)**
Establish the objectives and processes necessary to deliver results in accordance with customer requirements

DO **– Now Clause 8 Operations (Was product realization clause 7)**
Implement the processes

CHECK – Now Clause 9 Performance evaluation (Was Measurement, analyses and improvement clause 8)

Monitor and measure processes against policies, objectives and requirements for the product and report the results

ACT – Clause 5 Now Leadership (Was Management responsibility clause 5)

Take actions to continuously improve the process performance.

Structure of Clauses based on ISO 9001:2015DIS Figure 1

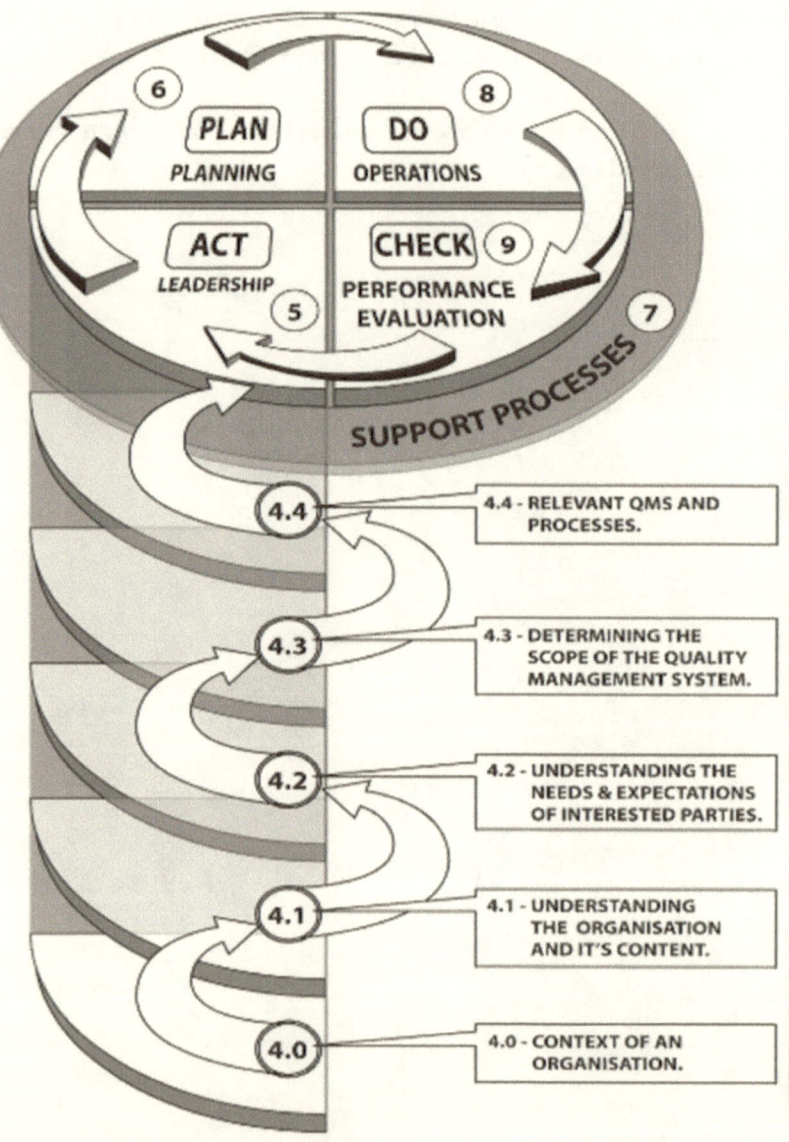

Note: - the **"Spiral of Scope"** covering the sub-clauses in **Clause 4 "Context of an Organisation"** are likely to cause concern as the changes within these clauses add many new terms. There are terms such as external issues, strategic direction, competitive, cultural, economic environment to name a few that need to be interpreted against the "Scope" of ISO 9001. The figure 1 In ISO 9001:2015DIS shows that the clauses 4.0, 4.1, 4.2 and 4.3 come through the centre of the circle up and into clause **4.4 relevant quality management system and processes** and then into **clause 5 Leadership** this is a significant change. Although the drawing is similar to the PDCA drawings shown throughout this document it does not have the clean approach shown within ISO 9001:2008 where each of the four clauses 5 – 8 cover the PDCA with clause 4 Management system surrounding the PDCA circle supporting it. This new approach highlights the responsibility of "Leadership" as they must deal with these issues.

NOTE: -It should be remembered that the new Annex SL structure is generic to many different standards and all should be interpreted against the scope of that particular standard. Clause 4.3 allows the organization to decide what the scope should include as it affects the ability to meet customer requirements. This then translates into the quality management system and processes required to meet the scope.

**The two figures below compare the two versions
<u>ISO 9001:2008</u>**

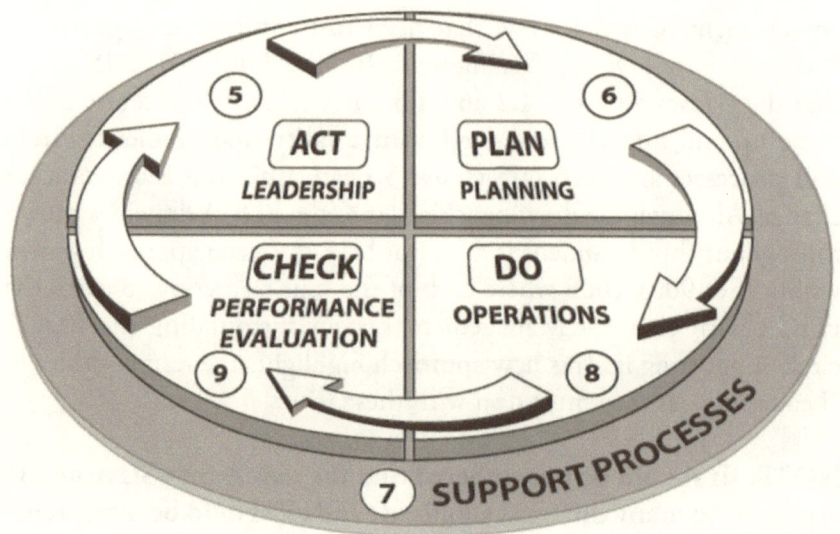

ISO 9001:2015DIS

ISO 9001:2015 Fig 1 indicates that the support processes only impact the "operations".

This is slightly modified in the above drawing as support processes cover all of the PDCA.

See "Spiral of Scope". Clause 4.4 Quality management system and processes is then led up into clause 5 Leadership (ACT).

It should be noted that: -

1. The current Clause 4.4 Quality management system and processes is now a sub clause where before it was a main clause that covered all of the organizations management system activities as they related to meeting customer requirements. This clause 4.4 now comes in under leadership. (See Figure 1 in ISO 9001:2015DIS)
2. The addition of sub-clauses to the figure 1 Model of a process based quality management system shows that the clause 4 Context of an organization covers: -

a. 4.1 Understanding the organization and its context
b. 4.2 Understanding the needs and expectations of interested parties
c. 4.3 Determining the scope of the quality management system

All coming out of the center of the PDCA circle and linking up to clause 4.4 as it goes into clause 5 leadership. (Covered by the spiral of scope below)

SPIRAL OF SCOPE (See section 2 Annex SL)

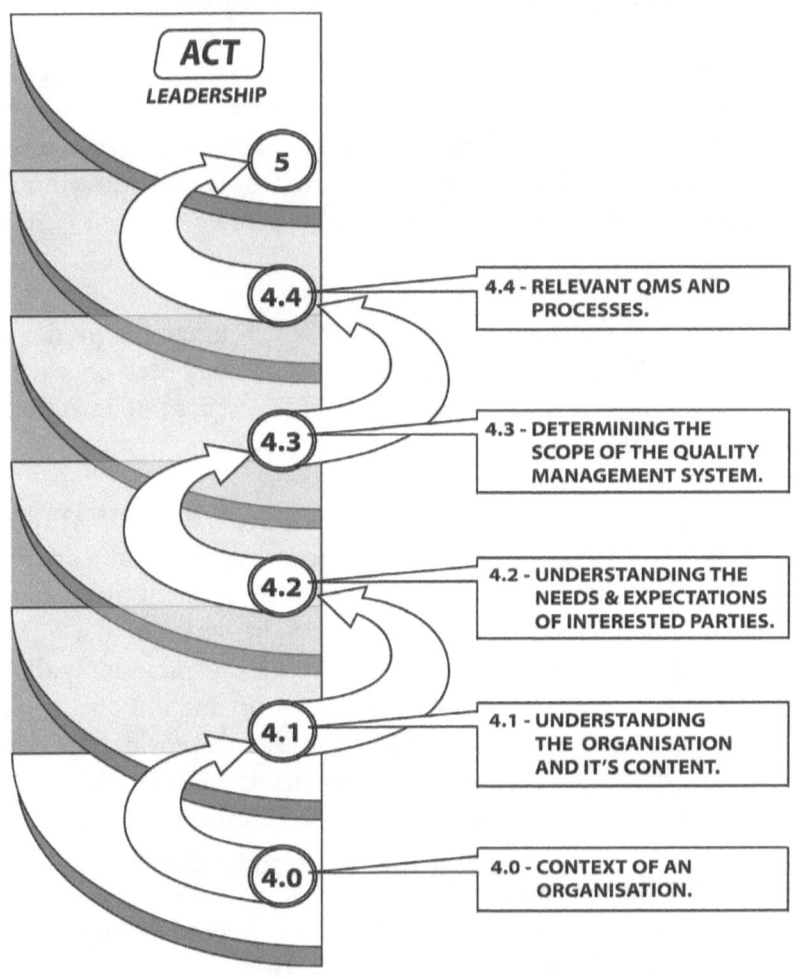

3. As the whole purpose of ISO 9001 is to provide the customer with the product or service they have specified it is hard to see that the requirement includes anything else as the scope specifically restricts itself to consistently meeting the customer and relevant statutory and regulatory requirements **unless** organisations themselves identify that other parties could prevent this happening.

As already mentioned it was the PDCA approach that drove the revision to the structure of the format in the 2000 version of ISO 9001. This was needed to ensure ISO 9001 did not just wait for things to go wrong.

> **Note:** - The ISO 9001 figure 1 (2015DIS) has now expanded the input from the Customer requirements (2008) to Customer and other **relevant interested parties.** The edition of **relevant interested parties** is where things could go wrong and will need to be controlled by each organization dependent on their business activities.
>
> If it is not understood who decides which interested parties are relevant there could be a problem. I have already been unofficially advised that this includes banks, insurance companies, local people, staff, local government etc.
>
> Unless it is clearly **understood** that it is the **ORGANISATIONS** responsibility to decide who the interested parties are and what risks are applicable then this could be difficult to manage. This is why clause 4.3 "Determining the scope of the quality management system" is so important to the organization. It **allows the organization to define what is relevant** and this only applies to what could affect their ability to consistently provide product or service that meets customer requirements. If this is not understood then it will allow "Subjective" issues to be introduced.
>
> **KEY 7.3 The most powerful tool to control and limit the possibility of subjective issues being introduced in ISO 9001:2015DIS is clause 4.3. This is because it is the responsibility of the "Organisation" to write an effective scope**

that would ensure their management system can consistently meet the customer specified requirements taking into account the restrictive role of ISO 9001. (See the Spiral of Scope)

0.4 **Plan, Do, Check, Act Cycle** is spelt out in ISO 9001 2015DIS has been modified with the Plan from PDCA shown in Figure 2 indicating that Plan – the process (Extent of planning depends on **RISK**) Surely that has always been the purpose of ISO 9001 to judge how the risks should be dealt with and putting in a management system that can consistently control the processes and meet customer requirements?

PDCA ISO 9001:2015 Draft with related Terminology and clause number

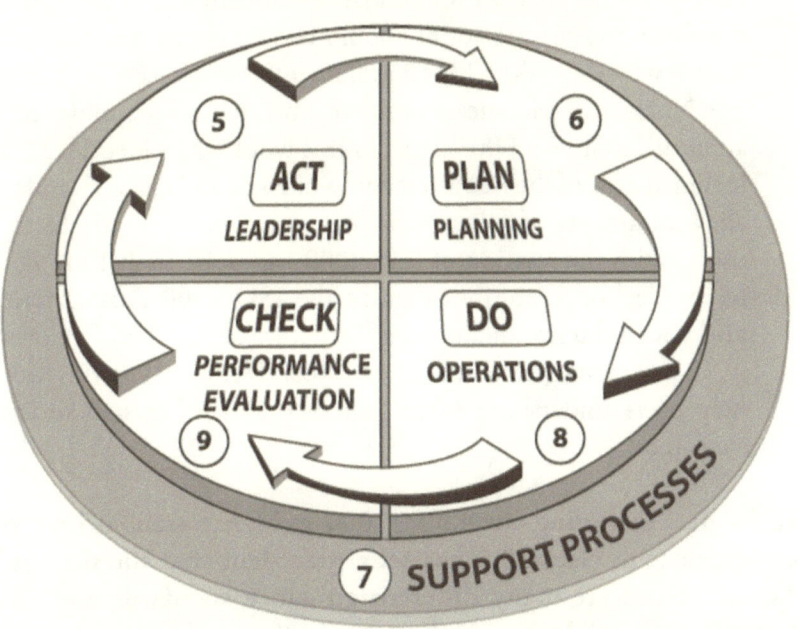

This shows the new terms in the same format as the similar diagram for ISO 9001:2008

The support processes above are shown to be across all of the activity not just operations.

Two clauses are missing clause 4 goes **into** Leadership and clause 10 improvement **exits** Leadership. This approach highlights the change in emphasis within leadership.

0.5 Risk based thinking is not a problem as long as it is restricted to the scope and purpose of ISO 9001 namely used to ensure the quality management system can consistently meet the customer requirements. In fact it is only stating what should already be taking place when implementing the ISO 9001 quality management system? The biggest error here is the inclusion of **ISO 31000 Guidelines on formal risk management** within clause 0.5. **This is a big mistake**. Bringing in one of the many Guidance standards by adding ISO 31000 will allow ISO 9001:2015 to be open to abuse and misuse "Risk" by itself is subjective. There should be no direct reference to any ISO Guidance standard as they are optional standards and organizations should choose if they are applicable. That is why ISO 9000:2015 Fundamentals and vocabulary should be a Normative reference identified as being "Indispensible" to the application of ISO 9001 2015 as this would, provided ISO 9000 included a list of the Requirement, Guidance and related standards, allow awareness of other standards to be readily available to all users. With the revision of ISO 9000 and 9001 in 2015 it would be an ideal opportunity to widen the **ISO 9000 Fundamentals and Vocabulary** to include the "Structure of Standards" (Covered in Clause 3 and Attachment A of this document) as this would help users understand what guidance and other standards are available.

KEY 7.4: - Including the ISO 31000 guidance standard on risk management in clause 0.5 has set a precedent that should not be allowed. There are many different guidance standards and all of them are optional. It is up to the organization to decide if they wish to use them. The structure of quality related ISO standards should be in ISO 9000.

KEY: - 7.5 ISO 9001:2015DIS Clause 2. Normative references indicates "There are no normative references" applicable? It is this failure to recognize the importance of the first three chapters of the

Requirement clauses namely Scope. Normative references and Terms and definitions and how they should be used that is of concern.

0.6 **Compatibility with other management systems** clearly indicates that ISO 9001:2015DIS that **Risk management** is **NO LONGER EXCLUDED even though ISO 9001:2008 specifically excluded RISK Management.**

(See ISO 9001:2008 Clause 0.4 Compatibility with other management systems states that risk management was excluded).

It is believed that "Risk Management" has been removed in ISO 9001:2015 DIS to enable the new Annex SL clause **6.1 "Actions to address risk and opportunity"** to be applied. The inclusion of "Risk Management", in its broadest meaning through mentioning ISO 31000 in clause 0.5, again highlights the confused message when it should be clear it is restricted to "Risk based thinking" against the scope of ISO 9001.

The current ISO 9001:2008 does not include risk management but this did not mean that risk was not applicable to ISO 9001 only that "Risk management", and all that entails, is outside the scope of ISO 9001. The term "Risk based thinking" is exactly what ISO 9001 management system was supposed to achieve.

Risk is SUBJECTIVE unless it is clearly linked to the **scope of ISO 9001** namely meeting customer requirements where it is totally **OBJECTIVE** provided the product and its specification are reviewed and understood before assessing the management system that is being used by the organisation. (See ISO 9001 Audit Trail attachment D)

KEY: - 7.6 The change from ISO 9001:2008 where Risk management was EXCLUDED to ISO 9001:2015DIS including "Risk and Opportunity" as a requirement clause is a "Risk" in itself. As long as the "Risk" is restricted to "Risk based thinking" it should not be a problem however if it is allowed to bring in Risk management and all that entails

through mentioning ISO 31000 it will be open to misuse. The whole purpose of ISO 9001 has always been to deal with risk as it relates to consistently meeting customer requirements.

The above is **NOT** trying to state that "Risk" is not relevant only that "Risk" has always been relevant and has to have been considered, when introducing an effective management system capable of consistently achieving the customer requirements.

How would it be possible to judge if a management system could consistently achieve the customer requirements if the risks of meeting customer requirements were not effectively dealt with?

8.0 Comparison between ISO 9001:2015DIS and ISO 9001:2008 requirements.

8.1 General

The first thing to recognise is that the "Scope" in ISO 9001:2015DIS (Draft International Standard) is the same as ISO 9001:2008.

The next thing is that ISO 9001:2008 and ISO 9001:2015DIS, having the same scope, **retains the restrictive role of ensuring that the organisations management systems is able to consistently provide product or service that meets customer and applicable statutory and regulatory requirements.**

Both standards cover "Improvement" and "Performance Evaluation" however ISO 9001:2015 has given these two requirements their own separate clauses.

The most significant change to clauses that have NOT been renamed is the failure to apply the clauses 2 Normative references and 3 Terms and definitions in an effective manner. (See definition section of this book for detail).

It is of concern that the current approach to revising ISO standards has led to a free for all regarding definitions, and revisions since 2011.

ISO 19011:2011 no longer identifies ISO 9000 as a 'normative reference', so the controlling standard for quality definitions is no longer referenced. Only 20 are defined under Clause 3 definitions and this has allowed standard terms to be missed out and resulted in multiple versions of what they mean.

This is not the only standard to ignore Clause 2 'normative reference' as the draft international standard (DIS) of ISO 9001:2015 and ISO 14001 have also not identified any normative references.

But what is the purpose of ISO 9000 fundamentals and vocabulary? It's the **core** standard within the ISO 9000 family of standards and the central repository for the definitions that relate to auditing and quality.

ISO 9000 FAMILY OF STANDARDS

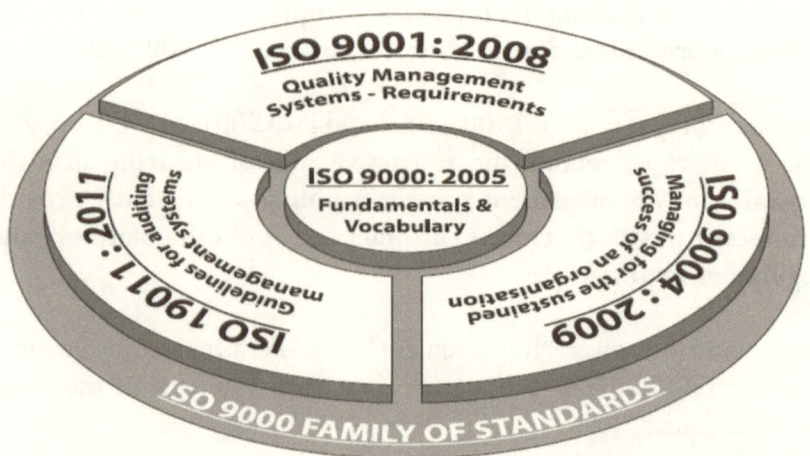

What is evident is that the first three clauses of ISO standards are generally ignored but they're important as they explain what the standard is about. But how should they be used?

The scope should be self-evident but ISO 9001 has a restrictive role clearly explained in the Clause 1 scope. Both standards have the same scope. The most common error is many do not know the statutory and regulatory requirements mentioned in the scope only cover the requirements the product or service being provided has to comply with.

ISO 9001:2008
Clause 2 'normative references' brings in ISO 9000:2005. Seeing as ISO 9000 calls up the ISO 9000 Family of standards, eight management principles along with 84 definitions so it should be understood.

ISO 9001:2015DIS
Clause 2 no normative references are called up

ISO 9001
Note: - Clause 3 'definitions' is where other definitions applicable to that particular standard can be introduced and it can even override a definition used in 'normative reference' by changing it to suit the needs of that particular standard.

ISO 9001:2008 Clause 3 definitions only states that where the term "Product" occurs it can also mean "Service".

ISO 9001:2015DIS has 69 definitions.

There is no need to put every definition in the standard but there should be one standard for each discipline that acts as the central control for definitions, and ISO 9000 is that standard and should be called up as a 'normative reference'.

ISO 9001:2015DIS has taken the same approach as ISO 19011 and I quote: -

"There are no normative references. This clause is included to maintain clause numbering alignment with other ISO management systems".

8.2 Summary of key differences (including elements from previous chapters)

KEY 8.1
The failure to recognise the important role of ISO 9000 has allowed many definitions to be changed without justification and ISO 9000 should be reinstated as a normative reference within ISO 9001:2015. (See ISO 9000 section in this book)

The ISO 9001 is still just one standard within a "Family of Standards" but from 2015 will consist of just three standards not the previous four. These three standards are to be termed the "Core" standards according to ISO 9001:2015DIS.

Note: - ISO 19011:2011 is going to be removed from the core "ISO 9000 Family of Standards".

KEY 8.2
Risk Management, which is specifically stated as NOT being applicable in ISO 9001:2008 clause 0.4, has been deleted from ISO 9001:2015CD and this is a significant change. This highlights the failure to recognize that ISO 9001 has a restrictive role and opens the door *to "Risk Management" which is by its nature subjective. There is an effort to reduce the Risk Management requirement to "Risk based thinking" however mentioning ISO 31000 within this clause is already causing confusion.*

KEY 8.3
To bring in a reference to ISO 31000 Guidance on Risk Management into the Risk Based thinking clause within ISO 9001:2015CD is setting a precedent. Indicting that ISO 31000 could be relevant to some organizations takes it outside the scope of ISO 9001 and makes it subjective. There are many issues that need to be addressed by an organization and that is why there are many ISO Guidance standards. Adding just one subjective guidance standard on risk is going to make ISO 9001 certification difficult if not impossible to interpret, control and manage.

KEY 8.4
The inclusion of some 69 definitions in ISO 9001:2015CD seems ill-conceived when this is the role of ISO 9000. This is especially relevant as there is NO index for the definitions in ISO 9001:2015CD and they are not in alphabetical order.

I am aware that this has been done because many organizations do not have IS0 9000 and people want everything in one document. So instead of teaching people that ISO 9000 is indispensable to the application of ISO 9001, as clearly stated in ISO 9001:2008 clause 2, we change the content of ISO 9001:2015DIS and include definitions.

Is this a logical reason to add definitions to every standard?

KEY 8.5
Bringing in the term "Interested Parties" may undermine the whole purpose of ISO 9001. The main interested parties covered by the scope of ISO 9001 are the organization and the customer. There could be others that can impact on the organisations ability to meet customer requirements however it is up to the organization to determine whether this will need to be taken into account or impact on their ability to meet customer requirements.

This will not be a problem if the "Spiral of Scope" is used effectively as the organization itself can control what is included within their own QMS scope (Clause 4.3)

KEY 8.6
ISO 9001 has not, and never has been, a standard that covers all of an organisations quality management system. (See chapter three of this book) Both the current (2008) and the new draft ISO 9001 have a restrictive role that covers the management system from agreeing with the customer what they require to delivering it to that agreed specification.

KEY 8.7
Including issues such as culture, external factors and social economic conditions could be just adding things that belong in ISO 9004. ISO 9004 is one of the "ISO 9000 Family of Standards" and deals with issues covering "managing for the sustained success of an organization" as stated in its title. In other words it covers all the issues beyond the restrictive scope of ISO 9001 that is why they are a "Family".

KEY 8.8
ISO 9001:2015DIS indicates that the quality management system of an organization will NOT have to change its structure providing it covers the relevant issues that affect their ability to meet customer requirements. As long as this is recognized by all parties the changes should not be too onerous.

KEY 8.9
The inclusion of strategic direction, needs and expectations of interested parties may expand the scope of ISO 9001 beyond its intended remit if the standard of advice given to organisation just continues the "Tick Box" approach of ensuring an organisations management system covers all clauses in the standard. It is important that the relevance of the clause 4 Context of the organization is assessed against the scope of the standard.

KEY 8.10
The decision to limit the ISO standards to highlighting the ISO 10000 series misses the opportunity to include and explain how other applicable quality standards should be structured and used. (See Attachment A and section 3 of this book)

Only including the ISO 10000 series of standards in ISO 9001:2015 restricts the information and it would be better if the information in attachment A was located in ISO 9000:2015 and that ISO 9000:2015 was identified as a Normative reference indicating that it is indispensable to the application of ISO 9001:2015.

KEY 8.11
Unless we improve the standard of auditing and teach auditors that they DO need to know what the specification for the product or service is when carrying out an audit we will continue to provide a sub-standard service.

8.3 Historical note on the ISO 9001 structure of clauses developed for ISO 9001:2000

The Plan, Do, Check, Act (PDCA) approach to the struture of clauses introduced in the year 2000 and increased the Measurement, analyses and improvement element by adding Preventive Action. Preventive Action was introduced to cover the "Vision 2000" findings where it was identified that previous ISO 9001 standards waited until something went wrong before taking any action. Unfortunately the term Preventive Action was incorrectly taught as meaning what happened when carrying out Corrective Action where the problems were prevented from happening again. This failure to understand the concept was compounded by using the term "CAPA" to cover Corrective and Preventive Action. Clauses 8.5.2 and 8.5.3 clearly explain the difference in the first sentence. Corrective action to prevent recuurance, Preventive Action to prevent their occurance.

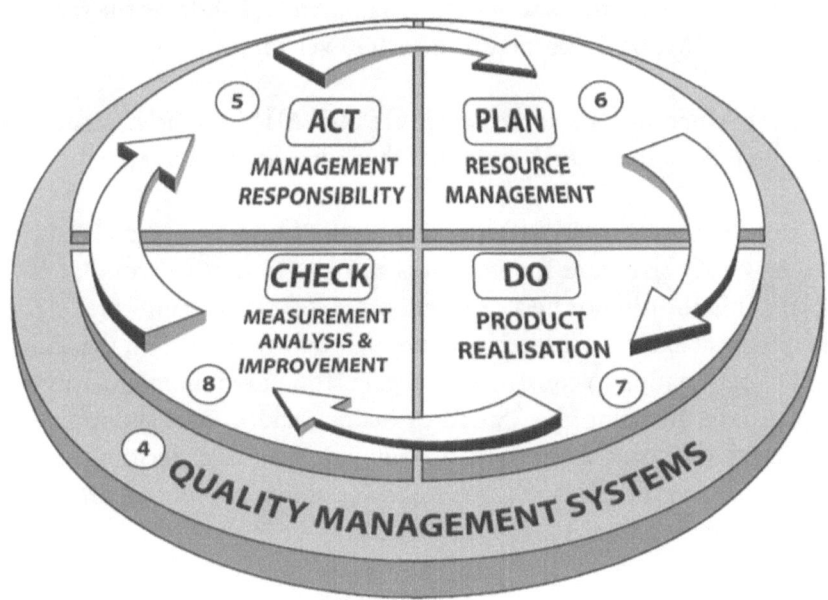

ISO 9001:2008 Version of Fig 1 including PDCA

Note: - Clause 4 Quality management system in ISO 9001:2008 is applicable to all the activities within the circle above

PLAN   – Clause 6 Resource management
Establish the objectives and processes necessary to deliver results in accordance with customer requirements

DO   – Clause 7 Product realization
Implement the processes

CHECK – **Clause 8 Measurement, analyses and improvement**
Monitor and measure processes against policies, objectives and requirements for the product and report the results

ACT – **Clause 5 Management responsibility**
Take actions to continuously improve the process performance.

In fact, as mentioned, it was the PDCA approach that drove the revision to the structure of the format in the 2000 version of ISO 9001.

However when we look at the new ISO 9001:2015DIS the structure has lost the link to the PDCA approach that formed the structure.

In fact ISO 9001:2015DIS has been revised to reflect the clauses of the new ISO structure for standards not the restrictive scope of ISO 9001. **This should not be a problem** provided that it is interpreted in a manner that excludes subjective issues that do not impact on the ability of the organization to consistently meet customer requirement. This can be achieved by using the "Spiral of Scope" taking each requirement, in clause 4 Context of an organization, in turn and deciding if it is applicable or will affect the organisations ability to consistently meet customer requirements.

It should be noted that ISO 9001:2008 **4.4 Relevant quality management system and processes** has been reduced to a sub clause within ISO 9001:2015DIS under the clause **4 Context of an Organisation**.

8.4 Spiral of Scope

This term has been introduced to try to explain the changes within clause 4 of ISO 9001:2015DIS. As mentioned the most significant change from the current ISO 9001:2008 is within clause 4 Quality Management System and clause 5 Leadership. Clause 4 has now been titled "Context of an Organisation". This change has reduced the current clause 4 Quality management system to a sub clause 4.4 entitled "Quality management system and processes".

This change has altered the 2008 clause 5 Management responsibility to Leadership as many new requirements have to be considered. The spiral of scope is trying to explain how this process may be managed.

SPIRAL OF SCOPE (See section 2 Annex SL)

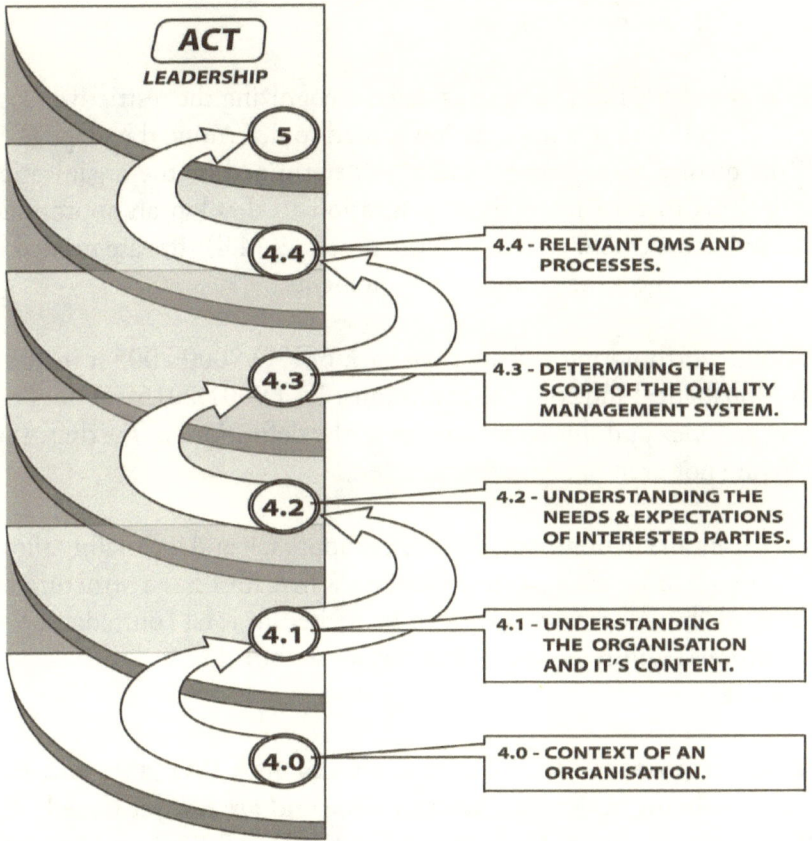

The Spiral of Scope illustrates how each section of clause 4 is examined to see if it is applicable or could affect the ability of the organisation to meet the customer requirements.

Clauses 4.1 and 4.2 covers: -

- Internal External issues
- Legal

- Technological
- Market
- Cultural
- Social
- Economic environments
- Needs and expectations of interested parties relevant to the QMS scope (4.3)

All of the above need to be considered recognizing the restrictive scope of ISO 9001 and this information is used to determine the scope (4.3) of the quality management system as determined by the organization itself. This in turn helps the organization to develop an appropriate quality management system and the processes (4.4) that are needed to consistently meet the customer requirements.

A point worth noting is that at the back of ISO 9000:2005 it includes an Alphabetical Index to the definitions. ISO 9001:2015CD does not have an index and this seems strange as the definitions in the draft ISO 9001are not even in alphabetical order?

It is hardly an environmentally effective approach and it certainly allows definitions to be changed in isolation. When ISO has a structure for standards but allows a standard to be revised in total contradiction to the purpose and structure of the clauses within that structure it does raise concerns.

Note: - It is not too late to correct this as both ISO 9001 and ISO 9000 are being revised at the same time and are not yet issued. The "Core" standards could all then reference ISO 9000 Fundamentals and vocabulary

9.0 Auditing

If we cannot or will not tighten up on the standard of auditing then quality will always be a poor relation to other management activity. The reason is from discussion with very senior personnel it is evident that the term "System Audit" has been introduced to allow the auditor to be told that they do not need to know what the product or specification for the product is as they are only doing a system audit

Note: - The term product in ISO 9001 can mean both product and/or service (Clause 3).

In fact the statement I have been given is: -

"ISO 9001 Certification is only about the organisation having a management system it is not about the auditor seeing if the system is effective as that is the responsibility of the organisation" Unquote.

When you read the scope of ISO 9001 the above approach will be seen as being totally ineffective in giving any assurance that the organisation can consistently meet customer requirements. (See ISO 9001 scope)

How can an ISO 9001 Certification audit give any confidence to the organisation and the buyer that their management system can consistently meet the customer requirements when the auditor does not know what the specification for the product or service is?

I have made government aware about this approach to auditing, where auditors audit the clauses of the relevant standard they are using and not the process itself. That is why auditing has now achieved such a poor reputation. If auditing only sees if the clauses in the relevant standard are covered in the auditees management system (Tick Box Audit) and fail to ascertain how effective the system is in consistently achieving the specified requirements auditing will never improve.

9.1 Professional auditing (See the book "ISO 9001 Audit Trail" for detail)

A professional audit is simpler and easy to carry out provided the auditor: -

a. Takes a selective sample of orders or contracts suitable to cover the scope of the audit.
b. Reviews the requirements for each of the chosen samples to understand the required output from each process.
c. Then with this information follows the selected samples for each order or contract chosen to ascertain if the management system is able to consistently meet the specified requirements.

Without understanding the output from a process it is not possible to judge if the quality management system is capable of consistently achieving the customer requirements. This requires a **process audit** following an **audit trail** of the samples chosen. Then as the output is known it is **totally objective**.

KEY 9.1 To enable audits to achieve their purpose it requires the auditor to carry out a process audit following an audit trail of the samples chosen. The auditor needs to takes a selective sample of orders or contracts, review the requirements for each of the chosen samples then follow the selected samples to ascertain if the management system is able to consistently meet the specified requirements.

9.2 ISO 9001:2015DIS

From reading the proposed new standard due to be released in 2015 there is ability to restrict the impact of some of the new terms such as: -

1. "Interested parties"
2. "Risk and Opportunity"

3. Legal, market, cultural, Social, Economic and many others where they are not relevant and will not impact on the organisations ability to meet its scope.

   This is where the "Spiral of scope" and clause 4.3 will help as it is the organisation that decides what is applicable. (See section 2 for detail)

9.3 Audit definitions

The concerns over the modification to definitions covering audit and audit evidence together with other issues is covered in section 11 Vocabulary and Definitions of this document.

However the definition for Auditor is worth mentioning here under auditing.

AUDITOR

2004
ISO 14001:2004
Person with the competence to conduct an audit

2005
ISO 9001:2005
Person with the **demonstrated personal attributes** and competence to conduct an audit.

This change looks quite good as it has added the need to **"Demonstrate personal attributes"**.

2011
ISO 19011:2011
Person who conducts audits

So in 2011 it was decided to remove both **"Demonstrate personal attributes" and "Competence" from the definition of auditor.**

2015 Draft standards
ISO 9001 and ISO 14001
Both of these drafts do not have a definition for auditor or call up ISO 9000 as a normative reference.

2015
ISO 9000:2014DIS does have a definition for auditor
Auditor: - Person who conducts an audit (the same as ISO 19011:2011) yet ISO 9000 is no longer a normative reference to the draft standards so the definition for auditor is lost.

If I was sceptical I would believe that the new definition is at least honest as it has removed competence as well as having suitable attributes. However, I believe it is an error made by concensus because the concerns raised above are not recognized as important. As a quality professional of decades of experience I believe it is my duty to raise these concerns and all I can say at this point is that everything in this book has been advised to the Chartered quality institute (CQI) in the UK, The International accreditation forum (IAF), International register of certified auditors (IRCA) as well as the United Kingdom Accreditation service (UKAS) and only the latter has deemed it important to respond and support some of my concerns.

I am, believe it or not, trying to help as I believe it is important to teach young auditors how to carry out professional audits that will add value to the organisation being audited.

9.4 Auditing definitions not yet defined

This is a sample from section 11 Vocabulary and definitions: -

A) **Audit Trail (Two drafts only as no definition has been approved): -**
1. An examination by a competent person, of an activity following the path that has been left by the process to ascertain if the management system is capable of consistently meeting the required outcome.
(Modified from the original definition PDQMS:2006)

2. systematic approach to collecting evidence based on specific samples, that the output of a series of interrelated processes meet expected outcomes.
(ISO 9001 Auditing Practices Group Audit trail December 2009)

B) **Observation**
An opportunity for improvement where something is identified that could help the organisation improve, but is not at that time a non-conformity.
(should be a benefit to the auditee)

KEY 9.2 – Two definitions should be added to ISO 9000:2014DIS if credibility is to be improved. They are "Audit Trail" and "Observation" these two fundamental terms are used when carrying out professional audits.

There is a need to add these definitions and despite IRCA inform issue 24 and ISO 9001 Auditing practicing Group (APG) (Attachment D) adding Audit Trail to their website in December 2009 there seems to be no support for introducing a definition for audit trail.

It is not possible to carry out an effective process audit without knowing what the outcome of the process should achieve and this approach undermines the credibility and illustrates how ineffective the auditing of the standard has become.

Within ISO 9001:2015DIS there are many definitions that have been modified and new definitions have been added. What is important is that ISO retains one definition for each term as this should prevent each standard writer applying their own version.

See section 11 Definitions section of this book

10.0 Improvement

This is the important difference between the pre 2000 version of ISO 9001 and the 2000 version. As already mentioned in the early 1990's there was a working group put together to identify what changes would improve the credibility of ISO 9001.

The working group was asked to ascertain the concerns regarding ISO 9001:1987 and this resulted in the 8 management principles.

Customer focus.
This was brought in because many quality professionals had been taught that it is the management system that is important and had ignored the needs of the customer.

Leadership
Many organisations brought in a quality manager and then left them to just retain their ISO 9001 certificate. In fact some managers thought ISO 9001 had little to do with the product and service that was being provided.

Involvement of people
This again was the recognition of the important role that people play in achieving the organisations purpose and how their abilities can be used to the benefit of the business

Process approach
It again recognised the importance of recognising that the benefits are achieved more effectively if the activities and related resources are managed as a process.

System approach
This covered the importance of identifying, understanding and managing the many interrelated processes as a system to ensure the organisations effectiveness

Continual improvement
This was brought in because one significant complaint about earlier ISO 9001 was they waited for things to go wrong before taking any action. This is why "Preventive Action" was introduced in ISO 9001:2000 to ensure that this concern was dealt with.

Factual approach to decision making
This pointed out the importance of gathering data and information upon which analyses could be used to help make effective decisions

Mutually beneficial supplier relationships
This highlighted that suppliers are quite crucial to the success of an organisation and when both worked together the benefits could lead to a "Win Win" situation.

Note: - Supplier relationships and responsibilities is also covered under use of sub-contractors

These 8 management principles are in ISO 9000:2005 and unfortunately a lot of training failed to recognise that ISO 9001:2008 and ISO 9000:2005 should be used as a **matched pair.**

ISO 9001 clearly stated that **ISO 9000:2005 is indispensable** to the correct application of ISO 9001:2008. (See clause 2. Normative references)

The work done by the working group in early 1990 eventually became known as "Vision 2000" and their findings were first published in 1993 when it became obvious to TC 176 members that to implement the improvement groups vision in the 1994 version of ISO 9001 would be too big a "Step" change as many other countries had just started to use the standard. It was then decided that the year 2000 would be a more appropriate date to implement the "Step" change hence "Vision 2000". The success of these changes allowed the standard to, with only minor changes, remain the same for 15 years

The structure of the 2000 version of the standard took the form of the Plan, Do, Check, Act approach (PDCA). So a quick reminder on PDCA.

PLAN: -being covered by 6.0 Resource management

DO: -being covered by 7.0 Product realization

CHECK: -being covered by 8.0 Measurement analyses and improvement

ACT: - being covered by 5.0 Management Responsibility

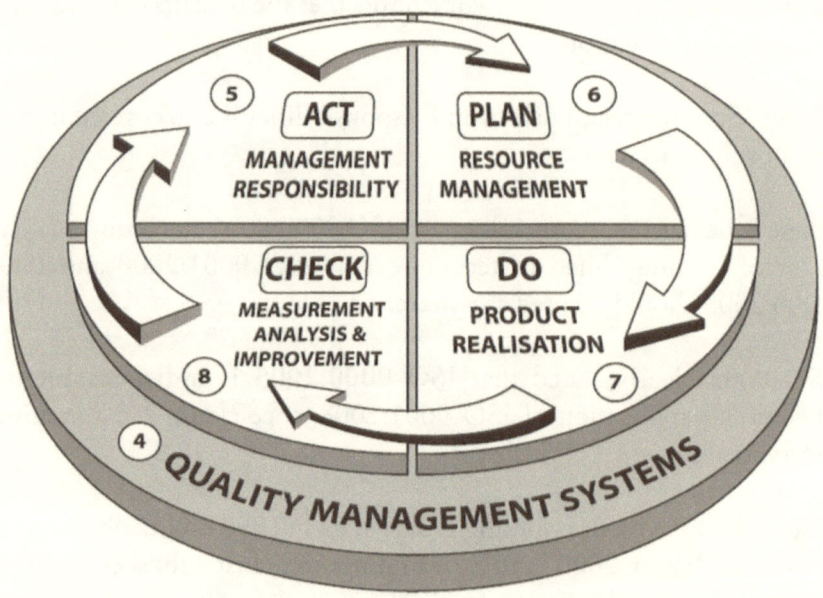

This allows an effective approach to quality management allowing the Plan, Do, Check, Act to influence the structure of the ISO 9001 standard. It has, at times, cause dissent as some people have indicated that some activities within clause 8.0 Measurement analyses and improvement should be in clause 7.0 Product realisation, however when the structure of the clauses and the logic behind it is explained they accept the compromise that had been made.

The Quality management system clause 4.0 of ISO 9001 covers how the above is managed.

This structure within ISO 9001 is very effective if it is used correctly.

It is worth noting that a QMS does not directly mean a documented management system.

(See Back to Basics 1 -10 Attachment B)

Too many people have been taught that you cannot audit a process unless it has a written procedure. This is nonsense and is recognized in ISO 9001:2008 by only requiring 6 procedures and allowing the organisation itself to decide what other documents and procedures they need. (ISO 9001 4.2.1 Refers)

So let us look at Improvement.

ISO 9000:2015 Draft defines improvement 3.3.1 as: -

IMPROVEMENT = ACTIVITY TO ENHANCE PERFORMANCE
ISO 9000:2015 AND ISO 9001:2015 DRAFT

The first thing to recognise is how to decide what needs improving and to do that you need **information.** This is where ISO 9000 comes in again.

INFORMATION = MEANINGFUL DATA
ISO 9000:2005, ISO 9000:2015 AND ISO 9001:2015 DRAFT

So where and when does an organisation gather meaningful data?

This is relatively simple if you have an effective management system that has implemented the ISO 9001 requirements applicable to the organisations needs

Let us look at the sources of information: -

- **Audits**
- **Logging "Correction"** that has taken place and the impact on the business
- **Analysing how effective "Corrective Action"** has been at removing the problem
- **Recording Preventative action** and its benefits and effectiveness
- **Develop Problem sheets (Attachment G)** identify and recording problems
- **Review all Problems (Attachment G)** obtaining information and analyse
- **Customer feedback** and whether they are satisfied or not
- **Monitoring and measuring** the effectiveness of processes
- **Monitoring and measuring the product**
- **Controlling non-conforming product** and investigating the cause
- **Analyses of the "meaningful" data**
- **Management reviews** where decisions can be made.

The above has been used for decades by effective managers however, too many times I have seen management reviews where the information presented at the management review is just "Raw" data that can give trends but does not provide information in a manner that can allow the organisation to take action.

An example I use when running a training course is as follows: -

Internal audits: -

In 2010 20 internal audits were carried out and 60 non-conformities were raised

In 2011 20 internal audits were carried out and 40 non-conformities were raised

In 2012 20 internal audits were carried out and 20 non-conformities were raised

My question to students following the above is "Do you believe this is information?"

Many indicate that they do think it is information. I disagree as my argument, which is often disputed, is it does not give "meaningful data" but just shows a trend.

When this is presented at management review managers congratulate themselves yet they have no real information. They have little information on what is causing the problems or whether the problems have just been corrected or completely removed. That being the case they cannot possible make sensible decisions on what "Actions" should take place that would allow them to ensure proposed changes and those changes already made have been dealt with in an effective manner ensuring that the problem does not reoccur.

To summarise when Information is supplied it should allow organisations and their management to make decisions based on this information to decide what needs to be implemented. Management need to appoint appropriate people with the relevant competence to achieve the task of eliminating the problem completely.

There are many tools that can be used to achieve this such as identifying the cost of the problem and using Pareto analyses to identify which problems are causing the most impact on the business and then implementing the improvement.

There are many quality Gurus such as Deming, Crosby, Juran etc who have put in place the processes and tools that can be used to help organisation improve.

All organisations have certain number of activities that have to be redone. Juran uses the term "Chronic Waste" to indicate where the same problem occurs over and over again. In many organisations it becomes accepted as being normal with no effort being made to remove the problems.

It is this failure to recognise that this waste of resources prevents organisations retaining their income. There is no point working hard to earn money and gain new business to find that, through your own failures, money is being wasted by having to carry out activities again.

The approach of the Quality Guru Deming and his PLAN, DO, CHECK, ACT is now clearly identified in the introduction to ISO 9001 page vi figure 1 the Model for process based quality management system.

(PDCA) is described as follows: -

Plan: establish the objectives and the processes necessary to deliver results in accordance with customer requirements and the organisations policies.

(CAN YOU DO IT?)

Do: implement the processes.

(DO WHAT YOU PLANNED TO DO)

CHECK: monitor and measure processes and product against policies, objectives and requirements for the product and report the results.

(GATHER THE INFORMATION ON HOW WELL THE PLAN HAS WORKED)

ACT: take action to continually improve the process.

(USE THIS INFORMATION TO DECIDE WHAT NEEDS TO BE IMPROVED AND ALLOCATE RESOURCES TO IMPROVE THE PROCESSES)

Not all organisations use the Plan, Do, Check, Act approach yet when you look at how it can be used to benefit the business it makes sense to implement it.

All organisations have to apply the "Plan and Do" approach and ISO 9001 covers this quite effectively as it encourages a clear understanding of what the customer wants and asks the organisation to be sure they have the resources and skills to be able to achieve that requirement. Within ISO 9001 is also asks them to plan how it will be carried out.

Where smaller organisations miss out is they don't gather information about the problems they have experienced. In fact they see it as being of no interest once the problem has been **corrected** they just move onto the next job. This misses out on the opportunity to take **corrective action** where the cause of the problem is identified and effort made to prevent it happening again. Corrective action is intended to prevent money being wasted by stopping the problem happening again. In fact in many cases it is this waste that reduces the profitability of the business.

It is worth mentioning the misunderstood terms used in ISO 9001.

From **ISO 9000:2005** they are: -

Correction 3.6.6
Action to eliminate a detected non conformity

This is where you just correct what has gone wrong. It can be as simple as providing the customer with a replacement product that is correct.

Corrective Action 3.6.5
Action to eliminate the causes of a detected nonconformity or other undesirable potential situation

This takes the issue further than **correction** by investigating why the problem occurred then taking action to ensure it does not happen again.

Note: -ISO 9001:2008 requires a procedure for this.

Preventative Action 3.6.4
Action to the cause of a potential nonconformity or other undesirable potential situation

This is used to ask organisations not to wait until things cause a problem but to encourage everyone to report anything they believe that could lead to a problem.

Note: - ISO 9001:2008 requires a procedure for this

These three terms are not always understood.

Correction is simple in that you just correct the error and that is allowed in ISO 9001 however it also requires you to carry out **Corrective Action** which means finding out the cause of the problem and doing something to stop it happening again.

Where the biggest confusion occurs is with **Preventative Action** as too many quality professionals do not understand that if a problem has already occurred then although you are being asked to prevent it occurring again that is NOT the meaning of **Preventive Action** as defined in ISO 9001.

This is quite clear if you actually read the definitions in ISO 9000.

Preventive action uses the term **"potential"** twice. **Corrective Action** states **"detected"**. In other words if some nonconformity has already been detected it is not covered by "Preventive Action". Preventive Action is only applicable **BEFORE** a problem has occurred.

This is quite clear if you recognise the importance of the Normative reference clause in ISO 9001:2008 where it states that ISO 9000:2005 is indispensable to the application of ISO 9001:2008. That is why I have on many occasions indicated that they are a **"Matched pair"** of standards. Even this statement is disputed by many quality professionals

As this book is aimed at the smaller to medium size businesses we will use a simple logical approach without complex methodology and terminology.

A technique I have used is the problem sheet. This is a simple A4 page similar to a Non Conformity Report that just captures information on problems (Attachment G).

To make the "Problem Sheet" stand out it is recommended that a coloured A4 paper is used and made readily available to all staff.

Literally it has a heading "Problem Sheet" with date, location and the person who filled it in.

The person who completes it can remain nameless if being anonymous helps get problem sheets completed.

It then has a space for the staff member or other to fill in what the problem was and if possible what impact it had on the job. This can be what it cost and or how much time was lost because of the problem. On completion this is then handed in to management or responsible party.

An example of this sheet is Attachment G.

This approach was used to capture defects over a specific Shut Down where I was advised that no one would fill them in. It was written in English on one side and the local language on the other using the same format both sides.

During this 4 week shut down over 100 Problem Sheets on light yellow paper were filled in. After analyses a direct loss of £250,000 plus an extra week added to the shutdown gave the information that could be dealt with. This waste was investigated and it was identified that ten of the problems caused a potential loss of £200,000.

This did not fit too well with the old 80/20 rule except regarding the costing however it met the principle of a small number of problems causing a large loss of both time and money.

Having this information allowed these issues to be prioritised using Pareto analyses and time was spent on Corrective Action on these 10 problem areas. These other problems were identified and some actioned however the 10 problems were the priority.

This was just one improvement process and it paid off as the next project was carried out on time and the losses were reduced to less than £ 75,000. (To those doing the maths new problems occurred) and benefited with a reduced time frame and smaller losses.

It was also identified that the most significant problem, that had caused the most losses, had occurred at least twice before and NO "Corrective Action" had taken place only "Correction".

These annual shut downs took place on a regular 5 year frequency covering the five similar units. (One shut down per year) In fact the time taken on each shut down was reduced because of this and other changes that took place having gathered the "Meaningful Data" (INFORMATION) and having accurate information.

The first thing to do, as already stated, is to identify the problem

PROBLEMS

This leads us back to the beginning of problem solving.

It is essential that a problem statement is written. This can then be part of the Quality Objectives that are set for the organisation. It does of course need the problem to be identified hence the use of "Problem" sheets as they identify what the concern is.

So it is necessary to decide what an effective problem statement is, and what is not.

Problem statements should only define the problem

PROBLEM STATEMENT

E.g. we have many instances where fitters are going out to the customer without all the equipment and tools they need to carry out the task.

This causes many man-hours to be lost as they have to return to the workshop or retail outlets to obtain the material required.

A method of checking if the problem statement is good is to score it against the following four elements: -

a) Is it a simple statement
b) Are numbers (Figures) provided
c) Is any background knowledge given
d) Are any costs given

The scoring is simple and like any good system you score each element of the problem statement so if the problem statement is good it would score 10.

To keep it simple we can score each of the four elements at 2.5 marks each.

Note: - you can weigh the scoring if you wish. (Say 4 marks for cost)

This is a simple method to judge if the above "Problem Statement" is good.

REMEMBER THIS IS REALLY JUST A BEST GUESS
Using the KIS approach (Keep it simple) let us look at the problem statement

   a) Is it a simple statement?
Yes it is simple and does give a picture of the problem
Score 2.0

   b) Are numbers provided?
This could be the number of times this occurs and currently there are no numbers provided
Score 0

   c) Is any background knowledge given
Yes it covers outside work however there may be other activities where this takes place
Score 1.5 or 2.0

d) Are any costs given?

No there are no costs or information about how much this is costing
Score 0

TOTAL SCORE

4 out of 10 so it is not such a good problem statement

What other "Meaningful Data" would help?

You could brainstorm this and see what comes up however for the purpose of the book we will add the types of things that would improve the problem statement.

Point b) Are numbers provided? What would you like to see?

For example over the last month there were 25 outside jobs carried out and 12 of them required people to leave the job site and spend time away gathering material

Seems useful however which month are we talking about as that would make it objective. Would it be useful to also identify the number of man hours required to tackle the 25 outside jobs? What percentage of time is being lost? Hopefully you get the picture

Point d) Are any costs given? What would we like to see?

Assuming that the man-hours spent away from the workplace gathering material added up to 12 hours over the month in question. Seems useful but what percentage of the total man-hours for outside work does this cover?

Again good data but what is it actually costing in pounds? Should we use an average hourly cost of £35. Total cost £ 420. Should this be gathered over a few months?

Hopefully you can see what would help.

So let's rewrite the problem statement

REVISED PROBLEM STATEMENT

We have many instances where fitters are going out to the customer without all the equipment and tools they need and carry out the task. This has caused 12 man-hours to be lost costing £420 in July alone as they have to return to the workshop or retail outlets to obtain the material and we have had customers complaints about the delay and in some cases we have had to go back the following day.

This is not a perfect problem statement but it is a little bit better than before as it does give some level of information and would allow the problem to be investigated.

We still don't know if this is across just two crews of two people or twenty crews of two people so there is still a lot of information needed. It is however better than the first problem statement.

An interesting fact is no support will be given unless the costs are put in money terms.

In fact many quality managers use the "Cost of Non-Conformity" termed (CONC). As this can often make managers sit up when they see the cost in £'s (CONC) and it then gets a reaction. The downside is all organisations have what "Juran" calls Chronic Waste. This simply means waste that goes on and on for ever as everyone ignores it. This is often where only "Correction" takes place not "Corrective Action" and is where the same problem reoccurs on a regular basis. This is often what is considered a small cost per incident but when it continues for years it adds up. That is why ISO 9001 is so keen on "Corrective Action" to remove this chronic waste. Even today many ISO 9001 Certified organisations only carry out "correction".

This is only a brief introduction and awareness of the benefits that could be obtained if the management system was set up to capture this information. Too many times people say they do not have the time to do this. This brings in the following statement

I DON'T HAVE ENOUGH TIME
TO DO THIS PROPERLY
BUT I ALWAYS HAVE ENOUGH TIME
TO CORRECT THE MISTAKES

As you can see this is just a basic introduction but when your organization automatically gathers information on where time and money are being lost it is not difficult to take action to remove these losses.

To all those quality professionals who may wish to ridicule this simplistic approach I will say it is not aimed at you but the many small to medium sized businesses to help get then started as many miss out improvement as they see it takes too long and is complicated.

Well it does not take a lot of time and it is not complicated.

In fact it takes minutes to fill in a problem sheet and when they are evaluated over a period of time it can give sound objective information. It is not even necessary to take action over every problem found all it does it allow you a choice. Simple common sense will let you decide if it is worth taking "corrective action". In some cases it will not but you decide if it would benefit the business.

I would suggest you try it. I did this in a country where I was advised it would not work and I can assure you it did. Even if just one organization uses this approach they will benefit by having information that they can work with to improve.

11.0 Vocabulary and Definitions

Within the four "ISO 9000 Family of Standards" the central core standard "ISO 9000:2005 Fundamentals and Vocabulary" has been defined as a Normative Reference in ISO 9001:2008, ISO 9004:2009 and ISO 19011:2002. It can also be used as a Normative Reference in other auditing and quality related standards as appropriate.

This approach ensured that there would be a common understanding of the quality and related vocabulary as they affect these standards. This is because ISO 9000 is the "core" central repository for audit and quality definitions. ISO 9000 retains the "Definitive" central control for Fundamentals and Vocabulary.

However since 2011 when ISO 19011 was revised the reference to ISO 9000 as a normative reference has stopped.

Key 11.1 Why was ISO 9000:2005 no longer called up as a "Normative Reference" in 19011:2011 "Guidelines for Auditing Management Systems?

The ISO standard Clauses, 2 Normative References and 3 Terms and Definitions, have a specific role in controlling this. It allows each standard to call on any other standard as a normative reference. In the case of Quality the ISO 9000 standard is used as a normative reference which allows a consistent approach.

Where a standard needs to use a definition that means something different or is new then clause 3, Terms and definitions, can be used to define the meaning for that **specific standard**. This allows flexibility yet retains the approved central control of definitions held in ISO 9000 to remain intact.

This practical and effective approach of calling up ISO 9000 as a normative reference is now being ignored. This started with the change of approach to ISO 19011:2011 Guidelines for Auditing Management systems where the revision of ISO 19011:2011 clause 2 Normative reference states: -

"No normative references are cited. This clause is included in order to retain clause numbering identical with other management system standards".

This seems to have ignored the logic behind the purpose and role of clauses 2 and 3.

ISO 19011:2011 actually has 20 definitions referenced in clause 3 and no normative references identified. The title of the standard is "Guidelines for auditing management systems" The previous version was titled "Guidelines for auditing quality and environmental management systems".

Having just 20 definitions in ISO 19011:2011 covering the "terms that relate to audit" from ISO 9000 when among the other 82 definitions in ISO 9000:2005 are Correction, Corrective Action, Preventive action, Audit Plan and Audit programme to name just a few that are now no longer covered. This is very strange when you recognise that the title of ISO 19011 is "Guidelines for auditing management systems"!

The revisions that are taking place do not use the ISO standard format for clause 2 and 3 in the manner intended. Here we have a guidance standard on auditing management systems that has thrown 62 definitions away. It has lost any continuity with its 2002 predecessor and instead of improving things has left things open, unclear and undefined.

KEY 11.2: - What is the purpose of removing 62 well established definitions from ISO 19011:2011 "Guidelines for Auditing Management Systems?

Is it the drive to make the standard generic beyond Quality and Environment that has undermined its role of "Guidelines for auditing management systems"?

To compound this error ISO 19011:2011 has also revised the definition for auditor.

ISO 9000:2005 Definition for AUDITOR is: -
3.9.9 Person with the demonstrated personal attributes and competence (3.1.6) to conduct an audit.

ISO 19011:2011 Definition for AUDITOR is: -
Person who conducts and audit (3.1)

Key 11.3: - The terms "demonstrated personal attributes" and Competence" in the ISO 9000:2005 definition of auditor have been removed from the definition in ISO 19011:2011 What is the justification?

This type of change is also evidenced with the change in the definition for **"Audit"** in ISO 9001:2015DIS.

ISO 19011:2011 3.1 Audit: - Systematic, independent and **documented process** for obtaining **audit evidence** (3.3) and evaluating it objectively to determine the extent to which the audit criteria (3.2) are fulfilled.

(The definition above is the same in ISO 19011:2011 and ISO 9000:2005 yet it has been revised in ISO 9001:2015DIS.)

ISO 9001:2015DIS 3.17 Audit: - Systematic and independent **process** for obtaining **objective evidence** (3.61) and evaluating it objectively to determine the extent to which the audit criteria (3.60) are fulfilled.

1st Concern: -
2005 mentions a **documented process** for obtaining audit evidence.

2015 drops **documented** and just mentions process yet ISO9001:2008 has a need for procedure (Documented) on Internal Audit. Has "Documented" been dropped as ISO 9001:2015 no longer requires any specific procedures?

2nd Concern: -
2005 mentions "**audit evidence**"
2015 calls it "**objective evidence**"

It is important to understand that "Audit evidence" covers everything that has been found during the audit. "Objective evidence" covers things that have been found that actually exist. In fact "Objective Evidence" is important when carrying out an audit as it ensures that auditors can write non conformities with clear indisputable facts. If necessary they can return to the specific item, location, and physically show what was found.

This seems to be a mistake as an auditor obtains **objective evidence** and **factual evidence** and these two terms form the **audit evidence**. (See below)

ISO 9000:2005 definitions: -
3.9.4 Audit evidence: - records statements of **fact** or other information which are relevant to the audit criteria and verifiable.

3.8.1 Objective evidence: - data supporting the existence or verity of something.

Note: - Objective evidence "data supporting the verity" (**truth**) of something whereas Audit evidence is - "records statements of **fact** that are verifiable.

ISO 9001:2015DIS definition: -
3.61 Objective/audit evidence - records, statement of fact or other information, which are relevant to the audit criteria and verifiable.

<u>**Key:-**</u> **11.4 ISO 9001:2015DIS has dropped the definition for Objective evidence indicating it is the same as Audit evidence and this is wrong.**

Note: - ISO 9000:2014DIS has two definitions for "objective evidence" (3.8.4 and 3.10.15) I can only hope that 3.8.4 objective evidence – data supporting the existence or verity of something is validated. It is essential that the belief that Audit Evidence and Objective evidence are the same is recognized as being untrue.

You will see from above that Audit evidence consists of "Objective Evidence" something that actually exists and "Fact" something that is true but may not physically exist. This evidence is then assessed against the audit criteria. From this the auditor decides what will be presented as Audit Findings.

An interesting situation has developed between the new draft ISO 9000 and ISO 9001 as ISO 9000:2014DIS still uses **"Objective evidence" (3.8.4) data supporting the existence or verity of something** yet ISO 9001 incorrectly indicates that objective evidence and audit evidence are the same by using the "Audit evidence" definition for both objective and audit evidence.

This is another example of where misunderstanding has taken place. The difference between **Audit evidence** and **Objective evidence** is quite simple. Audit evidence is all the information an auditor obtains. This can be a simple **fact** such as a form is no longer used. Objective evidence however has to have something that exists to support the truth (Verity) of something. If a form is no longer used then there is no objective evidence as you cannot see the form that is not used however an auditor will spend time to ensure the form is indeed no longer being used to ensure that "fact" is correct.

This belief that "Audit Evidence" and "Objective Evidence" are the same incorrectly modifies the definition for "audit". Even the definition used in ISO 9001:2015DIS 3.61 "obtaining objective evidence and evaluating it objectively" has incorrectly used objective to explain objective. Why it has changed "Audit evidence" to indicate it is the same as "objective evidence" within the section (3.10.1) definition for audit is hard to understand.

The three terms **Audit Evidence**, **Objective Evidence** and **Audit Findings** all have a specific role. (see above) The auditor obtains Audit Evidence containing Objective evidence, indisputable physical evidence, together with factual information, that is true, but no evidence exists then evaluates this against the audit criteria to develop the audit findings that are presented at the closing meeting.

The definition for "Audit findings" is the same in all three standards ISO 9000:2005 ISO 19011 and ISO 9001:2015 and this begs the question why does it have to be repeated in both ISO 19011 and ISO 9001 when ISO 9000 could be referenced in the Normative reference of these standards removing any confusion?

The above concerns are just two examples of where changes have been made to definitions that are not justified. No attempt has been made to consider all the changes that have been made however it is hoped that this will highlight the need to **verify** and **validate** that the changes made from ISO 9000:2005 are beneficial and necessary.

Currently because ISO 9001:2015DIS only has definitions in clause 3 and they only refer to ISO 9000:2014DIS there is no cross reference to the ISO 9000:2005 definitions so that changes can be easily identified.

11.1 Revisions to procedures and standards

The author has been carrying out Quality, Environmental and Health and Safety Management training and audits for decades. Within this training he makes it very clear how the changes to procedures or standards should be managed.

A particular issue that needs to be addressed is when a procedure or standard is revised it must be written for the benefit of the user not the benefit of the writer.

Within this approach it is important to ensure that changes from the previous version are identified and highlighted.

A method of doing this would, in any effective management system, be clearly defined in the **Document Control procedure** as that is its purpose.

There are many recognised methods such as highlighting the changes in bold or italics even putting a line down the margin of the text or underline it where it has changed.

An example of where this would help is in the definitions.

There are 84 definitions in ISO 9000:2005 and some 250 definitions in ISO 9000:2015DIS. *So there are many new definitions. It would be easy, in the index of* definitions, to put a letter (N) for new in brackets by the definition to highlight this.

(The above four lines illustrate how it is possible to identify where change has taken place)

Alternatively where a definition has the same title yet the content has changed it could be identified by a letter (M) for modified in brackets. Where no change has occurred it could be left unmarked. This approach would take little effort yet help the user.

The above is a simple basic quality approach that should be known by any competent quality professional yet no such approach has been taken with the revisions to ISO standards.

Where considerable change has taken place, say in the text, then it may be impossible to mark the changes however with the definitions this would be a simple and very easy and beneficial thing to do.

It has always been understood that a review of any standard was carried out to see if the standard was effective, needed modification or needed to be deleted.

The biggest problem with ISO 9001 is if it is not applied in a consistent manner some proposed changes may make this even more difficult to understand.

The current ISO 9001:2008, as it stands, can achieve its purpose and scope if it is used in an effective manner however the need to alter the structure of the standard so that all certification standards can use a common structure should be (Annex SL)

Note: - The author support the changes to the structure using Annex SL provided it is applied in a manner that helps the organization consistently meet the scope of the relevant standard namely, for ISO 9001, consistently meeting customer requirements.

Key 11.5: - The changes made to definitions in both ISO 9000:2014 and ISO 9001:2015 should clearly indicate if the definition is new, the same or has been modified compared with ISO 9000:2005 and should not be references against ISO 9000:2014DIS a standard not yet issued.

This failure to identify changes that have been made from the previous version ISO 9000:2015 does not help the user understand what has been modified.

Key: 11.6: - The approach of having no index and all 62 definitions in section 3 Terms and Definitions of ISO 9001:2015DIS when the

definitions are not in alphabetical order make using this section difficult. (There is no index)

This now leads us to ISO 9001:2015DIS where the same approach has been taken as ISO 19011:2011 by stating that: -

"There are no normative references. This clause is included to maintain the clause numbering alignment with other ISO management systems".

This raises the question over whether the purpose of the ISO standard clause 2 Normative references and clause 3 Terms and Definitions is understood by committee members?

This time ISO 9001:2015DIS has put some 69 definitions in clause 3 Terms and definitions dismissing the need to identify ISO 9000 as a "Normative reference".

Considering there are 82 definitions in ISO 9000:2005 it seems as if just a few definitions have been dropped however this is not true.

In taking a sample of definitions from ISO 9001:2015DIS and comparing them with 50% of those in ISO 9001:2005 it was noticed that ISO 9001:2015 has modified 12 definitions, 16 are new, 5 are no longer listed and 9 are the same. This indicates the change has been significant but not necessarily an improvement.

There is a problem with this approach as it is now possible to have many different definitions for each term within the ISO Standards. There is no longer a single definitive place in which definitions can be defined and kept.

ISO 9001:2015DIS has taken the same approach as ISO 19011:2011 having declined to reference any standard within clause 2 normative references. It is too late for ISO 19011:2011 yet it is not for ISO 9001:2015DIS and it is strongly recommended that ISO 9000 "Quality management systems – Fundamentals and Vocabulary" is identified as a Normative Reference within ISO 9001:2015.

Key 11.7 The failure to reference ISO 9000 as a normative reference in both ISO 19011 and ISO 9001:2015DIS is a big mistake as it allows definitions to be dropped without recognising the importance of having a single "Master" standard holding these definitions even if they are not relevant to that particular standard.

The correct approach would allow new and modified definitions to be included in ISO 9000:2015 together with the definitions that are unchanged. Then only those that need to be highlighted or have been modified should be included in ISO 9001:2015 clause 3 Terms and Definitions and ISO 9000 2014 would retain its "Core" role.

It would of course require ISO 9000:2014 to be identified as a normative reference in clause 2 of ISO 9001:2015. This allows a structured approach to the revisions and does not change the current use of the "Core ISO 9000 Family of Standards".

It will also allow those terms not mentioned in ISO 9001:2015DIS to still be retained as a referenced definition in ISO 9000:2014 even if considered not relevant to ISO 9001:2015.

I must admit the failure to include definitions for "Record, re-grade, release, auditor and specification" in ISO 9001:2015 is surprising. Maybe the term "Auditor" has not been defined because there are at least three versions in existence and one would have to be chosen? (See Auditor in ISO 19011:2011, ISO 14001 and ISO 9000:2005).

I am sure that I have missed some important issues as there is no index to the definitions in ISO 9001:2015DIS and they are not in alphabetical order and this has made this review difficult and time consuming.

It is important to recognise that the definitions in IS 9000:2005 are indispensable to the use of ISO 9001:2008 and many other quality standards. (See ISO 9001:2008 Clause 2.0)

If the International status of standards is to be retained common definitions should be used. Having a situation where each standard writer can develop their own definition is counterproductive. In fact the previous ISO format for standards allowed for variations where clause 2.0 Normative References allowed the standard to reference other standards e.g. ISO 9001:2005. Yet where a specific definition was unsuitable clause 3.0 could be used to introduce or rewrite a definition of that particular term for that specific standard or even introduce a definition that helps the reader understand a specific term.

KEY 11.8 for the credibility of quality standards a common definition should be used by all quality professionals. The most effective place to introduce this is in ISO 9000 as it is one of the "ISO 9000 Family of Standards" to be called the "Core" standard if the 2015 draft is approved.

The definitions below should be formally introduced to ISO 9001. (Wording can be changed)

a) **Audit Trail (Two drafts only as no definition has been approved): -**
   1. is the technique used by competent auditors of taking a selected sample of products then following the path that has been left by that process to judge if it can consistently meet the specified requirements.
   (From original definition PDQMS: 2006)
   2. systematic approach to collecting evidence based on specific samples, that the output of a series of interrelated processes meet expected outcomes.
   (ISO 9001 Auditing Practices Group Audit trail December 2009)

b) **Observation**
   An opportunity for improvement where something is identified that could help the organisation improve, but is not non-conformity.
   (should be a benefit to the auditee)

There is a need to add some definitions and despite IRCA inform issue 24 and ISO 9001 Auditing practicing Group (APG) adding Audit Trail to their website in December 2009 there is no support for introducing a definition for audit trail.

The fact that it is not possible to carry out an effective process audit without knowing what the outcome of the process should achieve undermines the credibility and illustrates how ineffective the standards have become.

Within ISO 9001 2015DIS there are many definitions that have been modified and new definitions have been added. What is important is that ISO retains one definition for each term as this should prevent each standard writer applying their own version.

In no way does this chapter cover all the issues that have changed as it is just a small sample used to illustrate how problems are being caused.

I apologize for the repetition within the above but feel strongly that having common definitions is important and identifying changes within standards would help users.

12.0 Conclusion

Please note that much of the discussion is over DRAFT standards and as such they are not relevant at present. However, it was felt that concerns raised now may be able to be recognized, agreed and modified in the final approved versions of the standards.

The revision to certifiable standards that is scheduled to take place over the next few years will include ISO 9001 Quality Management, ISO 14001 Environmental management, and ISO 45001 Occupational Health and Safety management (OHSAS 18001) as they will all be using the same Annex SL structure.

This book has used ISO 9001 as the example to explain how this new Annex SL structure could be implemented.

ISO 9001:2015DIS has retained the same scope as ISO 9001:2008 and that is good.

However some issues within ISO 9001:2015 have been misunderstood so the conclusions below highlight important issues that must be recognized if ISO 9001 is to ensure its scope and purpose is understood and applied in an effective manner.

The views expressed throughout the book are those of the author who as a quality professional of many decades experience feels it is important to share his concerns in the hope that the changes being made will improve the use of ISO standards to the benefit of the user.

1. The revision to the structure of certifiable ISO standards against Annex SL should be beneficial as it will allow organisations that wish to be certified to more than one standard to benefit from easy integration of those standards into their management system.
2. ISO 9001 benefits from the fact that ISO 9001:2008 and ISO 9001:2015DIS both have the same scope and that scope is restricted to the ability of the quality management system being

able to consistently achieve the customer requirements and improve.
3. A big concern is the removal of the term "ISO 9000 Family of Standards" (FoS) where ISO 9000:2005 makes it clear that ISO 9001 is just one standard within the family of standards and as such has a restrictive scope.
4. The second concern is the failure to call up ISO 9000 as a Normative reference. This is because ISO 9000 has been indispensable to the application of ISO 9001 for decades. The revision to ISO 9001 and ISO 14001 has disregarded the purpose of ISO standard clauses 2 and 3 by indicating that they have **no normative references** identified.
5. The purpose of ISO 9000 being the "Core" standard within the "ISO 9000 Family of standards" is to ensure that there is **one "Definitive" central location for fundamentals and vocabulary.**
6. **Changes made to definitions should be justified not just altered and separately introduced into each individual standard.** It would be beneficial to see the justification for any changes that have been made to the ISO 9000:2005 definitions. There are now 3 definitions for auditor and the definition for auditor is not included in ISO 9001:2015. The definition for **Audit Findings and Objective evidence is now believed to be the same.** This is one of many changes that are incorrect.
7. There are concerns but also opportunities to improve the understanding of how ISO 9001 should be used. (see Key highlights Attachment E)
8. There is a need to improve and have a common understanding of ISO 9001 Certification audits. Auditors should take a selective sample of orders/contracts, find out what the requirements are for those orders/contracts and carry out process audits following the audit trail to ascertain if the management system is able to consistently achieve the customer requirements
9. Each organisation should recognise that they have control of what is relevant to their management system as this control is within the sub-clauses of clause 4 of ISO 9001:2015. This is explained in detail through the "Spiral of Scope".

10. Remember ISO 9001 is totally **objective.** The proof of its effectiveness is that the organisation can consistently meet customer agreed requirements
11. The use of clause 3 "Terms and definitions" to include all the definitions instead of clause 2 Normative references has **allowed many different definitions for the same term to be introduced** and even some to be omitted or misused.
12. If the definitions in both ISO 9000 and ISO 9001 in **2015 do not identify which definitions are new (N) and which have been modified (M)** then it will not be complying with normal quality management revision processes.
13. It appears that the purpose of the revision of these two standards has been the need to apply Annex SL. This in some instances has led to just **"CHANGE" not improvement as two terms that should be defined if auditing is to become more effective, "Audit Trail" and "Observation"** have failed to be included despite being formal requirements for training auditors and being recognized by ISO 9001 Auditing Practices Group (APG) since December 2009. (See Attachment D)

FINALLY Please recognize that I am a concerned professional and not an author but for 5 years I have tried to get those in authority to go "Back to Basics" and understand where quality is failing to achieve its potential. Unless we recognize that we need to improve what takes place and not just rewrite standards or procedures we will make little progress. In fact we could make things worse so please forgive my humble effort to get people to stop and think and where I have made errors recognize I am only trying to help.

Kind Regards and Best Wishes for 2015

David John Seear

Any feedback good or bad please send to daveseear@btinternet.com

Attachment A

Number and issue	Type	Title	Status
		ISO AND OTHER RELATED SERIES OF STANDARDS	
	NOTE:-	THIS IS JUST A SAMPLE LISTING OF STANDARDS IT DOES NOT COVER ALL STANDARDS. THERE IS ALSO A NEED TO CHECK THE CURRENT ISSUE AND DATE FOR EACH STANDARD	
"CORE STANDARDS"		ISO 9000 Family of Standards	
ISO 9000:2005	"C"	Fundamentals and vocabulary	
ISO 9001:2008	"C"	quality management System Requirements	
ISO 9004:2009	"C"	Managing for the sustained success of an organisation- A quality management approach quality management approach	
"REQUIREMENT"	Tier 1	ISO REQUIREMENT STANDARDS	
ISO 10012:2003	R	Measurement management systems Requirements for measurement processes and measuring equipment	
ISO/TS 16949:2009	R	Quality management systems - Particular requirements for the application of ISO 9001:2008 for automotive production and relevant service parts organisations	
ISO 15378:2006	R	Primary packaging materials for medicinal products - Particular requirements for the application of ISO 9001: 2000 with reference to Good manufacturing Practice (GMP)	

ISO/TS 16949:2009	R	Quality management systems - Particular requirements for the application of ISO 9001:2008 automotive production and relevant service part organisations	
ISO/IEC 17021	R	Conformity assessment - Requirements for bodies providing audit and certification of management systems	
ISO 13485:2003	R	Medical devices - Quality management systems - Requirements for regulatory requirements	
ISO 28000:2007	R	Specification for security management systems for the supply chain	
ISO/CD TS 29001	R	Petroleum petrochemical and natural gas industries - Sector specific quality management systems - Requirements for product and service supply organisations	
ISO/IEC 27001:2005	R	Information technology - Security techniques - Information security management systems requirements	
"RELATED" REQUIREMENTS"	Tier 3 RR	OTHER NATIONAL AND INTERNATIONAL MANAGEMENT STANDARD REQUIREMENTS (INDUSTRY SPECIFIC)	
BS EN 12798:2007	RR	Transport quality management system - Road rail and inland navigation transport. Quality management system requirement system requirements	
ISO 14001:2004	RR	Environmental management system - Requirements with guidance in use	

BS EN 9100:2009	RR	Aerospace series. Quality management systems - Requirements (based on ISO 9001:2000) and Quality Systems. Model for quality assurance in design, development, production, installation and servicing (Based on ISO 9001:1994)
ISO 22000:2005	RR	Food safety management systems - Requirements for any organisation in the food chain
OHSAS 18001	RR	Occupational health and safety management systems - Requirements
"GUIDANCE"	Tier 2	GUIDANCE STANDARDS
ISO 10001:2007	G	Quality management - Customer satisfaction Guidelines for codes of conduct for organisations
ISO 10002:2004 Cor 1 2009	G	Quality management - Customer satisfaction - Guidelines for complaints handling in organisations
ISO 10003:2007	G	Quality management - Customer satisfaction - Guidelines for dispute resolution external to organisations
ISO/TS 10004:2010	G	Quality management - Customer satisfaction - Guidelines for monitoring and measuring Customer satisfaction
ISO 10005:2005	G	Quality Management Systems - Guidelines for quality plans
ISO 10006:2003	G	Quality management systems - Guidelines for quality management in projects
ISO 1007:2003	G	Quality Management Systems - Guidelines for configuration management

ISO/AWI 10008	G	Quality Management - Customer satisfaction - Guidelines for business to consumer electronic
ISO/TR 10013:2001	G	Guidelines for quality management system documentation
ISO 10014:2006 Cor 1 2007	G	Quality management - Guidelines for realising financial and economic benefits
ISO 10015:1999	G	Quality management - Guidelines for training
ISO 10019:2005	G	Guidelines for the selection of quality management system consultants and use of their services
ISO 19011:2011	G	Guidelines for auditing management systems
DD CEN/TS 15224:2005	G	Health services. Quality management systems - Guide for the use of EN ISO 9001:2000
ISO 1516:2001	G	Guidelines on the application of ISO 9001:2000 for the food and drink industry
ISO/TR 10017:2003	G	Guidance on statistical techniques for ISO 9001 2000
ISO/CD 10018	G	Quality management - Guidelines on people involvement and competencies
ISO 22006:2009	G	Quality management systems - Guidelines for the application of ISO 9001:2008 to crop production

ISO/IEC 90003:2004	G	Software engineering - Guidelines for the application of ISO 9001:2000 to computer software
ISO/IEC NP 90006	G	Information technology - Guidelines for the application of ISO 9001:2000 to IT services management
ISO/IEX TR 90005:2008	G	Systems engineering - Guidelines for the application of ISO 9001 to system life cycle processes
IWA 2:2007	G	Quality management systems - Guidelines for the application of ISO 9001:2000 in education
IWA 4:2009	G	Quality management systems - Guidelines for the application of ISO 9001:2008 in local government
TickIT Guide (5.5)	G	A guide to software quality management system construction and certification to ISO 9001:2000

The above is an illustrative example showing some of the standards that exist. It does not cover all standards that may be applicable

Attachment B

BACK TO BASICS LINKEDIN QUESTIONS

10 things were raised November/December 2013

Back to Basics 1. Can we now accept that the statutory and regulatory requirements called up in ISO 9001:2008 are only those requirements that the Product or service has to comply with?

This caused a lot of disagreement. ISO 9001 Scope restricts its role to consistently providing product that meets customer and applicable statutory and regulatory requirements. It goes on to state in Note 1 Product only applies to the product intended for or required by the customer. The word applicable above restricts the Statutory and Regulatory requirements to the product. Clause 3 also reminds people that where the term "product" occurs it can also mean "Service". So the statutory and regulatory requirements are only those requirements applicable to the product or service provided to the customer.

Back to Basics 2. Can we accept ISO 9001 does not include requirements specific to other management systems such as those particular to environmental, health and safety, financial and risk management.

ISO 9001:2008 clause 0.4 states: "This International Standard does not include requirements specific to other management systems, such as those particular to environmental management, occupational health and safety management, financial management or risk management." This was raised to remind people of the restrictive scope of ISO 9001 and how "Risk" is not applicable. With the revision to ISO 9001:2015 proposing a clause of Risk and Opportunity this will confuse things.

RESPONSE TO FEED BACK Some people do not accept that adding risk to ISO 9001:2015 is a problem. They state "Risk Based Thinking" is important. If it is just Risk Based thinking as it relates to the restrictive scope of ISO 9001 there would not be a problem. In fact ISO 9001 has been developed to help organisations address "Risk" in their processes to enable them to consistently meet their customer's requirements. My concern is that having "Risk" as a requirement will just be another clause that will be audited as part of the "System Audit" (Tick Box) approach with no real benefit. I do recognise that there is inherent risk in everything my concern centres around including a mention of ISO 31000 "Risk Management" and the term "Opportunity" in clause 6 as these are totally "Subjective" where effective use of ISO 9001 is totally "Objective". Having "Risk" as a requirement cause without explaining the restrictive scope of ISO 9001 will allow abuse and increase misuse by both certification bodies and consultants unless it is restricted to the scope of ISO 9001. If you fail to recognise the restrictive role of ISO 9001 as defined in "ISO 9000 Family of Standards" it will make things worse. (NOTE: - Opportunity has no role within the scope of ISO 9001)

Back to Basics 3. Can we accept that the primary purpose of ISO 9001 is to allow organisation to demonstrate that their management system can consistently meet their customers' requirements and improve?

This was stated as being just my view yet this is taken directly from the scope of ISO 9001 where it states that ISO 9001 specifies requirements for a QMS where an organisation a) needs to demonstrate its ability to consistently provide product that meets customer and applicable statutory and regulatory requirements. b) Including processes for improvement of the system to ensure conformity to customer and applicable regulatory requirements concluding with Note 1: - goes on to explain that a product only applies to the product intended for the customer.

Back to basics 4 Can we accept that a quality management system (QMS) does not directly equate to a documented management system?

This is also quite straight forward in that ISO 9001 itself only requires 6 procedures and then refers to 4.2 documentation requirements where 4.2.1 states "Documents, including records determined by the organisation to be necessary to ensure the effective planning, operation and control of its procedures". The "Key element is documents determined by the "Organisation" no one else.

RESPONSE TO FEED BACK more people now agree in principle however too many auditors have been told they cannot carry out an audit unless there is a procedure. This has led to the current bureaucratic documented systems. I don't have any problem with the statement that the amount of documentation needed to control the process might be affected by the "RISK" however cannot accept that putting more documentation in will remove the Risk. This is incorrect as effective resources and competent people can be equally effective if not more so.

Back to Basics 5 Can we accept that ISO 9001 Certification should assure organisations and their customers that the organisations QMS is capable of meeting the customer's requirements

This has been difficult as many people indicated that an ISO 9001 cannot assure anything. This is where I do not agree. ISO 9001 certification can't guarantee that the organisation will always provide product that meets the customer's requirements however a professionally carried out audit should be able to demonstrate that the organisation has an effective management system that should enable it to consistently meet the customer's requirements. This cannot be achieved unless the Auditor knows what the specification for the product is.

If they do then it allows the audit to be totally objective and the QMS can be judged against its ability to meet the customers' requirements.

Back to Basics 6A Can we accept that the purpose of an audit is to see if a process is effective and achieves the desired result whether it be a 1st party (Internal), 2nd party (Supplier/Vendor) or third party audit (External)?

This caused some disagreement as different scopes were mentioned. What I was attempting to do is get agreement that all audits are process audits to see if the QMS can achieve the intended output.

RESPONSE TO FEED BACK I have agreement that people understand what I am saying. A response talked about calibration and the checking of the measuring equipment however I always teach my students not to just audit Calibration, Training and other single clauses as all audits should be against the processes. To audit calibration a sample of jobs going though at the time should be chosen then the relevant instruments being used should be checked to ensure they meet the ISO 9001 requirements. Internal Audits when carried out by competent auditors could be more effective than 2nd or third party audits provided they are carried out against a selected sample of work going through at that time using competent knowledgeable auditors. There is a tendency to add issues into "Internal audit" such as efficiency and that is fine if that is what the organisation wished to include within the scope of their Internal Audits. I would however remind you that "efficiency" is outside the scope of ISO 9001. It is this addition of things because it is important without considering the restrictive scope of ISO 9001 that allows the confusion to continue. As I have stated organisations can use the clauses in ISO 9001 to help them across all of their business activities but that should NOT allow the scope of ISO 9001 to be extended without proper controls and understanding.

Back to Basics 7A (Audits) Can we accept that ISO 9001 certification audits should cover the management system processes that directly affect the ability of the organisation to meet product specification?

Originally "B2B" 7 stated "Should just cover the QMS" and I was corrected and the change made as shown. I agreed there were other issues that needed to be covered. What I had tried to convey is that the primary process is to ensure the QMS is capable of consistently meeting the customer requirements. My concern being that many auditors do not take the time to find out what the specification for the product actually is so cannot achieve this primary purpose. (See Below)

Back to Basics 8 (Audits) can we accept that ISO 9001 Certification auditors should take the time to find out what the product and specification for the product is before carrying out an audit?

Once again some disagreement as the people who had been taught that ISO 9001 auditors do not need to know what the product or the specification for the product is when doing an ISO 9001 audit did not agree as they have been taught the "System Audit" approach where auditors do not need to know what the specification for the product is because they are only auditing the "System". My argument is surely the system should achieve something (see the ISO 9001 scope).

RESPONSE TO FEED BACK There has been some agreement however there seems to be a view that I am basing my views on traditional manufacturing and that is incorrect. I have covered Hospitals, Training and even government offices all of which I have been involved with. The response mentions the Characteristics of the product that are important to the customer. That is clearly defined in what is agreed between the customer and the organisation. What is happening is that some quality professionals are bringing in ISO 9004 requirements and this takes ISO 9001 beyond its scope making it subjective.

Yes it is important for the organisation to consider what the customer wants and the design, where appropriate, does cover this and yes it includes (Stated, implied and obligatory) as well as applicable statutory and regulatory requirements as they relate to the product/service being provided. From what has been stated if the revision to ISO 9001:2015 is not carefully managed it will broaden the role of ISO 9001 making it subjective. ISO 9001 as it stands is quite clear and totally "Objective" provided the auditor knows what the processes should achieve, as it only covers what the customer and organisation have agreed and any auditor worth the name will take a selective sample find out what the customer requires and audit to see if the QMS in place is adequate to achieve that requirement.

Back to Basics 9 (audits) Can we accept that all audits should be process audits following an audit trail to ascertain if the process can consistently meet the specified requirements?

This is a fundamental requirement if credibility is to be achieved. Just auditing to see if a procedure is followed is not good enough. The whole purpose is to see if the management system can consistently meet the customer's requirements by following a selected sample of orders.

This is agreed in some quarters however once again arguments against has mentioned the traditional manufacturing context and large one off Manufacturing construction project/service sector situations software and educational organisations yet that is exactly what ISO 9001 covers. Using ISO 9001 is quite effective provided it is used by competent professionals who have not been misled over how ISO 9000 and ISO 9001 (The matched pair) should be used. (See ISO 9001 clause 2 where it states ISO 9000:2005 is indispensable to the application of ISO 9001)

Back to Basics 10 "IMAGINE" that the 9 "Back to Basics" are true. If the auditor selected a sample of orders, found out the agreed requirements, did a process audit to see if the QMS could meet those requirements would this give auditing more credibility and benefit the auditee?

Finally the above was put out to allow people to think about what the standard actually states rather than just repeat what they have been led to believe. In other words look at the 9 "Back to Basics" to see if ISO 9001 actually states what they have been told. It is a reminder that ISO 9001 has a restrictive role that only covers the QMS that directly relates to the product or service involved.

The possible cause of this confusion is the failure of many trainers to advise trainees that ISO 9000:2005 is indispensable to the application of ISO 9001. In fact many certified organisations have little or no knowledge about ISO 9000 despite this being a clear requirement defined in ISO 9001 clause 2 Normative References.

Note:-
ISO 9001 CERITIFICATION DOES NOT, AND SHOULD, NOT ATTEMPT TO COVER ALL QUALITY ISSUES THAT AFFECT THE ORGANISATIONS ACTIVITIES.

HOWEVER THE CLAUSES WITHIN ISO 9001 MAY BE USED ACROSS ALL THE ORGANISATIONS ACTIVITIES PROVIDED IT IS RECOGNISED WHEN ACTIVITES ARE OUTSIDE THE SCOPE OF ISO 9001.

Attachment C

SUMMARY OF CONCERNS RE ISO 9001 REVISION 2015

RAISED AT CQI LEADERSHIP CONFERENCE 1ST April 2014

As a quality professional of many decades experience I feel it would be remiss of me not to highlight my concerns.

I would like to point out a few issues that seemed to have slipped through the net and may undermine the future effectiveness of the "ISO 9000 Family of Standards" especially the revision to ISO 9001 in 2015 as this will affect its ability to provide objective certification.

The current version of ISO 9001 is already subject to inconsistent interpretation.

> A main concern is the use of the term "System Audit". Many auditors are advised that it is not necessary to know what the product or specification is. How this can give any assurance that the organisation can consistently achieve the customer's requirements when they don't know what the specification for the product or service is. This approach concerns me as it undermines the credibility of the quality profession.
>
> This led to the need for a definition for "audit trail" being developed one example is in the www.iso.org/tc176/ISO 9001AuditingPracticesGroup (see Attachment D) in 2009 and there is still no indication that this term, mentioned 4 times in IRCA guidance for auditor training, will be defined.
>
> The introduction of the term "Stakeholder" or "Interested Party", the latter being the preferred term in ISO 9000:2005, is cause for concern as ISO 9001 only has two core interested parties they being customer and organisation. The "ISO 9000 Family of Standards" explains this.

I am advised that the term "preventive action" is to be removed because it is not understood. This would appear to be a "Knee jerk" reaction, why not ensure it is used correctly? Bringing in "Risk and Opportunity" to replace it could cause even greater confusion than using "preventive action". The primary purpose of ISO 9001 is to mitigate risk from agreeing with the customer what is wanted to delivering the required product or service.

Introducing "Risk" will make ISO 9001 subjective unless the term "Risk" is restricted "Risk based thinking" as it applies to the restrictive scope of ISO 9001 namely to have a management system that can consistently meet the customer's requirements.

I accept that "Risk and Opportunity" is in Guide 83 the task is to ensure the text within this clause reflects "Risk" as it applies to the scope of ISO 9001. Opportunity is not relevant as it outside the scope.

In trying to understand the level of confusion surrounding the use of ISO 9001 a series of questions were raised into the LinkedIn forum during November and December 2013. The responses are available today at this Conference. The document is titled "Back to Basics LinkedIn Questions".

(See Attachment B)

My concern is that the changes that are proposed to ISO 9001 will be influenced by the new structure for ISO standards Guide 83. (Now known as Annex SL) This should not be a problem provided all clauses, regardless of the purpose and scope of the standard being revised, restricts the activity to the scope of the standard.

If the scope of both ISO 9000 and ISO 9001 are not fully understood this could lead to the proposed changes being defined by the German word "Verschlimmbessern".

This word is from: -

Verbessern "To improve" and Verschlimmern " To make worse"

The reason I am pointing this out is that unless the role and purpose of the "ISO 9001 Family of Standards" are understood and the scope of the ISO 9000 Family of Standards retained it may well lead to things becoming more confused by adding subjective issues into ISO 9001.

Finally I would add that the revised Terms and Definitions in ISO 19011:2011 has changed the definition for auditor to "Person who conducts an audit" removing "attributes" and "competence" from the ISO 9000 2005 definition 3.9.9. "person with the personal attributes and competence to conduct an audit" this gives me cause for concern regarding the changes being planned for ISO 9001:2015.

I am only trying to help and I hope the above points give all parties food for thought.

PDQ Management Services e'mail daveseear@btinternet.com or go to www.pdqms.co.uk

Attachment D

International Organization for Standardization   International Accreditation Forum
Date: 10 December 2009

ISO 9001 Auditing Practices Group Guidance on:

Audit Trail

The following paper by David John Seear is adapted from an article in IRCA's INform journal (Issue No.24, December 2009, http://www.irca.org/inform/issue24/Seear.html)

1. Introduction

There are numerous important elements to carrying out a professional audit. Some requirements, such as the need to audit the process, are defined in ISO 9000. There is, however, one element of auditing that is missing in the terms and definitions in ISO 9000 – the ***audit trail***.

The failure to carry out a process audit following an audit trail is the single most important reason why audits are not effective.

2. What is an audit trail?

In the absence of a definition from ISO 9000, a standard dictionary definition for 'audit' and 'trail' arrives at the following:

A systematic approach to collecting evidence based on specific samples, that the output of a series of inter-related processes meets expected outcomes.

But what does this mean in practice?

Although applied by some auditors, the use of an audit trail is by no means universally accepted. It is the failure to ensure all audits employ process audits following an audit trail that undermines their credibility. Auditors should understand the path of the process that they are auditing and perform the audit accordingly, ensuring that the requirements of the process are being met.

For example, as a matter of course auditors will visit the shop floor. This enables the auditor to see what is taking place and to identify the specific order numbers of jobs that are going through at that time. From this information it is easy to identify in the sales department the agreed specification for that product or service and select relevant samples to be chosen. This means the process can be checked to ensure that what takes place is controlled and will meet the required specification. From here, the audit trail is picked up and followed through.

Using the audit of a purchasing activity as an example, you need to identify what material or equipment has been purchased for your sample order. It is always important to understand what drives the process. In this case, it is normally the requisition, which defines what is wanted.

If the auditor does not understand the specification, then he or she cannot check if the process being followed meets the requirements of the requisition.

- what does the requisition require – does this comply with the agreed specification?
- how is the decision to purchase made?
- how is the specification decided? Is it adequate?
- who decides what is required and do they have the authority?
- who chooses the supplier and by what criteria?
- what is the process for bid evaluation?
- how is the specification advised to the supplier?

- are national or international standards used?
- what controls the process?
- are there any special packing delivery requirements?

These are just some of the issues that need to be addressed, many of which follow the clauses of ISO 9001.

3. Correct samples

The starting point for the audit is to use the chosen samples and identify the process path and the controls that were applied. It is vital that the samples are linked and come from the same trail. Too frequently, audit samples are taken at different stages of the process and are not related or linked to the initial sample chosen, which means that an auditor is unable to verify that the process is working. He will only be able to check if that particular document is filled in correctly.

Procedures, forms, checklists and so on, all ensure that a process is managed and controlled effectively. It is essential that auditors take the time to understand what is required from the process they are auditing.

It is impossible for a second- or third-party auditor to carry out an audit of an organization if the auditor does not take the time to understand the specification of its product or service, including statutory and regulatory requirements. It is this professional approach to auditing that allows the auditor to identify any weaknesses in the process and decide if an organization is capable of meeting the specified requirements. The audit trail approach applies to any audit be it an internal, second- or third-party audit.

About the author

David John Seear C. Eng. (daveseear@btinternet.com) spent 12 years at sea, where he reached the position of Chief Engineer, followed by 20 years with Shell UK, where he was appointed as 'Head of Quality and Performance' for Shell UK Materials. He represented the UK on ISO /TC176 for 3 years, as well as representing the Confederation of British Industry on the UK's mirror committee to ISO/TC 176. He now runs PDQ Management Services.

For further information on the ISO 9001 Auditing Practices Group, please refer to the paper:

Introduction to the ISO 9001 Auditing Practices Group

Feedback from users will be used by the *ISO 9001 Auditing Practices Group* to determine whether additional guidance documents should be developed, or if these current ones should be revised.

The other ISO 9001 Auditing Practices Group papers and presentations may be downloaded from the web sites:

www.iaf.nu
www.iso.org/tc176/ISO9001AuditingPracticesGroup

Disclaimer

This paper has not been subject to an endorsement process by the International Organization for Standardization (ISO), ISO Technical Committee 176, or the International Accreditation Forum (IAF).

The information contained within it is available for educational and communication purposes. The *ISO 9001 Auditing Practices Group* does not take responsibility for any errors, omissions or other liabilities that may arise from the provision or subsequent use of such information.

Attachment E

STRUCTURED SELECTION OF KEY ISSUES

There are many "KEY" issues that have been raised within this document covering four distinct areas: -

- "Back to Basics"
- "Possible Detrimental changes"
- "Things to be aware of"
- "Opportunities for improvement

The number of "Key" issues has been reduced and presented using the above structure to better present the concerns in a structured manner.

The **KEY** number itself allows reference back into the text to see why it was raised.

Back to Basics
1. KEY 1.1 - It is true that the tools, (Clauses) within ISO 9001 may be used by the organization across all of their management activities however, when it is used beyond the restrictive scope of ISO 9001 it can cause confusion. The failure to understand and recognize when ISO 9001 is used outside its intended scope causes misunderstanding.
2. KEY 1.2 - The primary purpose of ISO 9001 certification is to allow both the organization and their customers to have confidence that the quality management system being used can consistently provide product or service that meets the customer/specified requirements.
3. KEY 1.3 - Making changes to ISO 9000 and ISO 9001 in 2015 without having a common understanding of their roles within quality may confuse rather than promote the benefits of quality. (See Attachment B, 10 Back to Basics questions)
4. KEY 1.4 - The quality profession should be able to demonstrate the benefits of an effective management system, without resorting to forcing subjective requirements onto ISO 9001 Certified organisations.

5. KEY 6.0 - ISO 9001 is one standards within the "ISO 9000 Family of Standards" and it has a role that is restricted to having a quality management system that can consistently meet customer requirements and improve.
6. KEY 6.2 - the statutory and regulatory requirements are only those requirements that the product or service has to comply with.
7. KEY 8.6 - ISO 9001 has not, and never has been, a standard that covers all of an organisations quality management system. (See chapter three of this book) Both the current (2008) and the new draft ISO 9001 have a restrictive scope covering the management system from agreeing with the customer what they require to delivering it to that agreed specification and improving the system.

Possible Detrimental changes
8. KEY 2.1 -The failure to reference ISO 9000 as a normative reference in ISO 9001 DIS removes the central repository for fundamentals and vocabulary.
9. KEY 5.1- Since 2011 new standards within the "ISO 9000 family of standards" no longer call up "ISO 9000 Fundamentals and Vocabulary" as a "Normative Reference". This makes it difficult to understand the purpose of ISO 9000? In fact the role of ISO 9000:2005 is to be the "Core" standard within the Family of standards. ISO 9000 retains the central "Definitive" control for fundamentals and vocabulary. When this is not used within the "ISO 9000 Family of Standards" it undermines the purpose and structure of the Family.
10. KEY 8.3 To bring in a reference to ISO 31000 Guidance on Risk Management into the Risk Based thinking clause 0.5 within ISO 9001:2015CD is setting a precedent. Indicting that ISO 31000 could be relevant to some organizations takes it outside the scope of ISO 9001 and makes it subjective. There are many issues that need to be addressed by an organization and that is why there are many ISO Guidance standards. Adding just one subjective guidance standard on risk is going to make ISO 9001 certification difficult if not impossible to interpret, control and manage

11. KEY 7.4 - Including the ISO 31000 guidance standard on risk management in clause 0.5 has set a precedent as there are many different guidance standards and all of them are optional. It is up to the organization to decide if they wish to use them. The structure of quality related ISO standards should be identified in ISO 9000. (See attachment A)
12. KEY - 7.5 ISO 9001:2015DIS Clause 2. Normative references indicates "There are no normative references" applicable? It is this failure to recognize the importance of the first three chapters of the Requirement clauses namely Scope. Normative references and Terms and definitions and how they should be used that is of concern.
13. KEY 8.1 The failure to recognise the important role of ISO 9000 has allowed many definitions to be modified without sensible justification. ISO 9000 should be reinstated as a normative reference within ISO 9001:2015. (See ISO 9000 section in this book)

Things to be aware of
1. KEY 2.2 -The clause 4.3 in the new ISO 9001 will allow each organisation to look at what, how and when the new terms such as Risk, Opportunity, Interested parties etc could impact on the organisations ability to consistently meet customer requirements. In doing this the organisation can adjust the scope 4.3 so it is specific to their business. (See the "Spiral of Scope")
2. KEY 2.3 Under no circumstances should any Organisation bow down to pressure to take action on every clause or phrase in ISO 9001:2015 where there is no benefit to the organisation itself.
3. KEY 2.4 ISO 9001:2015 clearly states that there is no need for an organisation to change its management system to follow the clause numbering of the revised standard. What the organisation needs to do is ensure the elements within each clause are covered as they relate to their business.
Elements that should be changed
4. KEY 7.2 - Changing the term from "ISO 9000 Family of Standards" to just the "Core" standards is one of the many things changed that have lost the link to the previous standard.

The term "Core ISO 9001 Family of Standards" might help retain the link to the past.

5. KEY 7.3 - The most powerful tool to control and limit the possibility of subjective issues being introduced in ISO 9001:2015DIS is clause 4.3. This is because it is the responsibility of the "Organisation" to write an effective scope that would ensure their management system can consistently meet the customer specified requirements taking into account the restrictive role of ISO 9001. (See the Spiral of Scope)

6. KEY 7.6 - The change from the ISO 9001:2008 where Risk management was EXCLUDED to ISO 9001:2015DIS including "Risk and Opportunity" as a requirement clause is a "Risk" in itself. As long as the "Risk" is restricted to "Risk based thinking" it should not be a problem however if it is allowed to bring in Risk management and all that entails through mentioning ISO 31000 it will be open to misuse. The whole purpose of ISO 9001 has always been to deal with risk as it relates to consistently meeting customer requirements.

7. KEY 8.2 Risk Management, which is specifically stated as NOT being applicable in ISO 9001:2008 clause 0.4, has been deleted from ISO 9001:2015CD and this is a significant change. This highlights the failure to recognize that ISO 9001 has a restrictive role and opens the door to "Risk Management" which is by its nature subjective. There is an effort to reduce the Risk Management requirement to "Risk based thinking" however mentioning ISO 31000 within this clause is already causing confusion.

8. KEY 8.5 - Bringing in the term "Interested Parties" may undermine the whole purpose of ISO 9001. The main interested parties covered by the scope of ISO 9001 are the organization and the customer. There could be others that can impact on the organisations ability to meet customer requirements however it is up to the organization to determine whether this will need to be taken into account or impact on their ability to meet customer requirements. This will not be a problem if the "Spiral of Scope" is used effectively as the organization itself can control what is included within their own QMS scope (Clause 4.3)

9. KEY 8.7 - Including issues such as culture, external factors and social economic conditions could be just adding things that belong in ISO 9004. ISO 9004 is one of the "ISO 9000 Family of Standards" and deals with issues covering "managing for the sustained success of an organization" as stated in its title. In other words it covers all the issues beyond the restrictive scope of ISO 9001 that is why they are a "Family".
10. KEY 8.8 - ISO 9001:2015DIS indicates that the quality management system of an organization will NOT have to change its structure providing it covers the relevant issues that affect their ability to meet customer requirements. As long as this is recognized by all parties the changes should not be too onerous.
11. KEY 8.9 - The inclusion of strategic direction, needs and expectations of interested parties may expand the scope of ISO 9001 beyond its intended remit if the standard of advice given to organisation just continues the "Tick Box" approach ensuring an organisations management system covers all clauses in the standard not how effective the processes are then it will undermine its credibility. It is important that the relevance of the clause 4 Context of the organization is assessed against the scope of the standard. (Spiral of Scope)
12. Key 10.1 - Why was ISO 9000:2005 no longer called up as a "Normative Reference" in 19011:2011 "Guidelines for Auditing Management Systems?
13. KEY 10.2 - What is the purpose of removing 62 well established definitions from ISO 19011:2011 "Guidelines for Auditing Management Systems?

Opportunities for improvement
2. KEY 3.1 - To ensure there is a clear understanding about the structure and terminology used within the numerous quality standards a listing of standards similar to Attachment A could be included in ISO 9000:2015 and this could be kept up to date and readily available through the internet.
3. KEY 3.4 - Tier 2 ISO structure of standards covers guidance documents and as such they are not a requirement and it is up

to the organisation itself to decide what guidance documents are beneficial.
4. KEY 8.4 - The inclusion of some 69 definitions in ISO 9001:2015CD seems ill-conceived when this is the role of ISO 9000. This is especially relevant as there is NO index for the definitions in ISO 9001:2015CD and they are not in alphabetical order.
5. KEY 8.10 - The decision to limit the ISO standards to highlighting the ISO 10000 series misses the opportunity to include and explain how other applicable quality standards should be structured and used. (See Attachment A and section 3 of this book) Only including the ISO 10000 series of standards in ISO 9001:2015 restricts the information and it would be better if the information in attachment A was located in ISO 9000:2015 and that ISO 9000:2015 was identified as a Normative reference indicating that it is indispensable to the application of ISO 9001:2015.
6. KEY 8.11 - Unless we improve the standard of auditing and teach auditors that they DO need to know what the specification for the product or service is when carrying out an audit we will continue to provide a sub-standard service.
7. KEY 9.1 To enable audits to achieve their purpose it requires the auditor to carry out a process audit following an audit trail of the samples chosen. The auditor needs to takes a selective sample of orders or contracts, review the requirements for each of the chosen samples then follow the selected samples to ascertain if the management system is able to consistently meet the specified requirements.
8. KEY 9.2 – Two definitions should be added to ISO 9000:2015DIS if credibility is to be improved. They are "Audit Trail" and "Observation" these two fundamental terms are used when carrying out professional audits.
9. Key 11.3 - The terms "demonstrated personal attributes" and Competence" in the ISO 9000:2005 definition of auditor have been removed from the definition in ISO 19011:2011 without clear justification?

10. Key 11.4 - ISO 9001:2015DIS has dropped the definition for Objective evidence indicating it is the same as Audit evidence and this is wrong.
11. Key 11.5 - The changes made to definitions in both ISO 9000:2015 and ISO 9001:2015 should clearly indicate if the definition is new (N), the same or has been modified (M) compared with ISO 9000:2005 and should not be references against ISO 9000:2014DIS a standard not yet issued.
12. Key: 11.6 - The approach of having no index and all 62 definitions in section 3 Terms and Definitions of ISO 9001:2015DIS when the definitions are not in alphabetical order make using this section difficult.
13. Key 11.7 - The failure to reference ISO 9000 as a normative reference in both ISO 19011 and ISO 9001:2015DIS is a big mistake as it allows definitions to be dropped without recognising the importance of having a single "Master" standard holding these definitions even if they are not relevant to that particular standard.
14. KEY 11.8 - for the credibility of quality standards a common definition should be used by all quality professionals. The most effective place to introduce this is in ISO 9000 as it is one of the "ISO 9000 Family of Standards" to be called the "Core" standard if the 2015 draft is approved.

Once again sorry about the repetition

Attachment G

PROBLEM SHEET

Location of problem ....

Name (Optional)..   Date ....

Problem – To be completed by anyone

Signed ....

CORRECTIVE ACTION PLANNED (To be completed by department manager and or quality manager)

Signed (For department) ....   Signed (Responsible party) ....

To be completed by: (Date) ....   Follow-up date ....

VERIFICATION (To be performed by auditor, giving details of checks made to ensure problem resolved)

Corrective action complete and satisfactory ....   Date ....

Attachment H

KEY HIGHLIGHTS

CONCERN 1
The failure to reference ISO 9000 as a "Normative reference" in ISO 19011:2011 is a major concern. The inclusion of some 69 definitions in ISO 9001:2015CD illustrates how the purpose of the "ISO 9000 Family of Standards" is misunderstood and the use of clauses 2, Normative References and 3, Terms and definitions has not been effective.

REASON
ISO 9000:2005 covers Fundamentals and vocabulary. This standard can and should be used as a normative reference for many auditing and quality standards. (E.g. ISO 9001, 9004 and ISO 19011 as well as ISO 14001). The approach of adding so many definitions to each new or revised standard fails to recognize that having one standard (ISO 9000) that acts as the authority for definitions prevents unauthorized changes. The approach being used now allows many different versions of a definition to exist. There are now 3 definitions for auditor. The failure to use clause 2 effectively is evidenced in ISO 19011:2011, ISO 9001:2015DIS and ISO 14001DIS where no Normative reference have been called up.

(See definitions for "auditor" in these three documents against ISO 9000:2005.)

CONCERN 2
Bringing in the term "Interested Parties" could, but should not, undermine the purpose of ISO 9001. This is because clause 4 Context of an Organisation brings in some issues that may not be relevant to the restrictive scope of ISO 9001. Normally the only interested parties covered by the scope of ISO 9001 are the organization and the customer. Where there are other parties that could affect their ability to meet customer requirements then they can be introduced.

REASON
"Interested Parties" include shareholders, banks, local councils, and neighbours etc, who are not relevant to the scope of ISO 9001. Some of these parties even have conflicting interests so how any Certification Body can assess if the organization can consistently meet the "Interested Parties" requirements will be totally subjective. There is however clause 4.3 determining the scope of the quality management system which will allow the organization to make the decision regarding what should be included.

CONCERN 3
ISO 9001 has not, and never has been, a standard that covers all of an organisations quality management system. (See chapter three of this book) ISO 9001 has a restrictive role that only covers the management system from agreeing with the customer what they require to delivering it to that agreed specification and improving.

REASON
Including issues such as culture, external factors and social economics conditions is just adding issues that belong in ISO 9004. ISO 9004 is a "Core" standard that deals with issues covering managing for the sustained success of an organization. In fact the Annex SL structure is more relevant to the whole of the "ISO 9000 Family of Standards" than just one of them.

CONCERN 4
The decision to limit the explanation over the structure of related ISO standards to ISO 10000 series misses the opportunity to include and explain how other applicable quality standards should be structured and used. (Attachment A)

Including this in ISO 9001 restricts the information and it would be better if the information was located in ISO 9000:2015.

REASON
There are many other standards such as "Requirement" and Guidance standards that are not easily identified or referenced.

CONCERN 5

The whole purpose of ISO 9000:2005 is to cover the fundamentals and vocabulary so that fundamentals and definition do not have to be repeated in every auditing or quality related standard.

REASON

To indicate in ISO 9001:2015 clause 2 that there are no Normative references yet follow it up with clause 3 Terms and definitions where 69 clauses are defined most of which cross refer to ISO 9000:2014 defeats the intention and purpose of these two clauses within the structure of a standard. In fact these definitions should be cross reference against ISO 9000:2005 definitions not a draft standard not yet issued.

CONCERN 6

The inclusion of some 69 definitions in ISO 9001:2015CD seems ill-conceived when this is the role of ISO 9000. This is especially relevant as there is NO index for the definitions in ISO 9001:2015CD and they are not in alphabetical order.

REASON

I am aware that this has been done because many organizations do not have IS0 9000 and people want everything in one document. So instead of teaching people that ISO 9001 cannot be used without having ISO 9000, as clearly stated in ISO 9001:2008, we change the content of ISO 9001:2015CD.

CONCERN 7

The inclusion of strategic direction, needs and expectations of interested parties expands the scope of ISO 9001 beyond its intended remit unless where they are not relevant to the scope they are excluded.

REASON

Too many quality professionals have failed to take into account the restrictive role of ISO 9001. In fact many complaints about ISO 9001 are not justified if the scope and purpose of ISO 9001 was understood. The way ISO 9001:2015CD is being applied could take the revised standard outside its scope and will make the assessment of the management system subjective.

CONCERN 8

Unless we improve the standard of auditing and teach auditors that they do need to know what the specification for the product or service is when carrying out an audit we will continue to provide a sub-standard service.

REASON

Since 2009 the author has tried to ensure that a definition for audit trail is included in the revision to ISO 9000. The whole purpose of revising a standard is to improve it. The approach taken so far would indicate that there is no concern over the standard of auditing. The failure to recognize that the auditors need to know what the expected outcome of a process should be if they are to judge if the management system being used is effective has been ignored.

CONCERN 9

To bring in a reference to ISO 31000 Guidance on Risk Management into the Risk Based thinking clause 0.5 within ISO 9001:2015CD is setting a precedent. Indicting that ISO 31000 could be relevant to some organizations takes it outside the scope of ISO 9001 and makes it subjective. There are many issues that need to be addressed by an organization and that is why there are many ISO Guidance standards. Adding just one subjective guidance standard on risk is going to make ISO 9001 certification difficult if not impossible to control and manage.

REASON

The need to go "Back to Basics" is essential. If we cannot agree about the scope and purpose of ISO 9001 and how the ISO 9000 Family of Standards should be used then we have no right to make changes that will affect over a million certified organizations. If we could ensure that certified organization have a management system that can consistently meet the specified requirements we would improve the standing of quality. Without a common understanding this will never be achieved.

CONCERN 10

Risk Management, which is specifically stated as NOT being applicable in ISO 9001:2008 clause 0.4, has been removed from ISO 9001:2015CD and this is a significant change. This highlights the failure to recognize that ISO 9001 has a restrictive role and opens the door to "Risk Management" which is by its nature subjective. There is an effort to reduce the Risk Management requirement to "Risk based thinking" however this terminology is already causing confusion

REASON

ISO 9001:2008 specifically stated that "Risk Management" was not applicable. This did not mean risk was not taken into account. In fact quite the contrary the whole purpose of ISO 9001 was to encourage organization to have an effective management system that removed any risk that could affect the organizations quality management systems ability to consistently meet their customers' requirements.

About the Author

David John Seear C.Eng CMarEng FIMarEST FCQI CQP is a chartered engineer who spent 12 years at sea ending up as Chief Engineer with a combined First Class Chief Engineers certificate before leaving and joining Shell U.K.

After 20 years at Shell UK, where he had been Quality Manager and Head of Quality and performance, for Shell UK Materials running the Quality and Performance department one of the three departments reporting to him was Quality Appraisal whose purpose was to carryout 2nd Party audits. He represented the CBI on BSI QMS 22 for 6 years and represented the UK on ISO 9000 TC 176 for three years

He has lived in Brunei and Abu Dhabi and carried out audits and training throughout the world including Africa, North and South America, Russia, Europe, Scandinavia, as well Singapore and Malaysia when he lived in the Far East and Pakistan, India, Jordan, Kuwait, Bahrain, when in the Middle East.

He is an IRCA Principal Auditor of 30 years experience and runs PDQ Management Services that carries out training, auditing, Consultancy and lecturing on various management issues especially procurement and supply chain management.

Email daveseear@btinternet.com

The Author

Quality above and below

Let this book be your co-pilot through the
changes in order that you do
not drown in terminologythat is not relevant
to your organisations business

David John Seear

www.ingramcontent.com/pod-product-compliance
Lightning Source LLC
Chambersburg PA
CBHW030804180526
45163CB00003B/1147